AWAY HAPPENS

For Lois with
love from

Peter + Jennifer

AWAY HAPPENS

Phil Crossman

⚓ ⚓ ⚓

University Press of New England

Hanover and London

Published by University Press of New England,

One Court Street, Lebanon, NH 03766

www.upne.com

© 2005 by Phil Crossman

Printed in the United States of America 5 4

ISBN–13: 978–1–58465–445–2

University Press of New England is a member of the Green Press Initiative. The paper used in this book meets their minimum requirement for recycled paper.

Library of Congress Cataloging-in-Publication Data
Crossman, Phil.
Away happens / Phil Crossman.
  p. cm.
ISBN 1–58465–445–7 (pbk. : alk. paper)
 1. Vinalhaven (Me.)—Social life and customs. 2. Vinalhaven (Me.)—
Biography. 3. Crossman, Phil. 4. Hotelkeepers—Maine—Vinalhaven—
Biography. 5. Community life—Maine—Vinalhaven. I. Title.
F29.V7C76 2005
974.1'53—dc22   2004024949

CONTENTS

PREFACE

The fullness of life on a remote Maine island is found in the nearly unavoidable interactions we who live here have with one another. It compares—sometimes favorably, sometimes unfavorably—with life elsewhere, but it is certainly a complete experience.

Vinalhaven is an island village in Maine, about fifteen miles from the mainland and accessible only by boat, state-run ferry, or air taxi. Its 1,276 people are sufficiently removed from the rest of the world as to occupy an insular environment in which we all work, play, love, and hate. Some of us travel extensively; others never leave the island. Still, when push comes to shove, as it often does, we live here with, and respond to, one another. We share and continually contribute to a mercurial body of common knowledge that is our community baggage, and therein we find our strengths and our shortcomings, our accomplishments and our misdeeds. We are compelled to endlessly consider ourselves in the context of others, and it is the time spent in such contemplation that gives our lives a wholeness (not to be confused with wholesomeness). More than anything else, though, we find a communal circuitry and involvement with one another whether we like it or not. Some of us clearly don't. Nonetheless, we're all players on this stage of forty or so square miles, and nothing in our lives is more present than familiarity.

Several years ago it was revealed to me that creative nonfiction was a legitimate literary genre. It was the most liberating experience of my life. All these years I thought I'd been simply lying. Most of these essays are examples of creative nonfiction. The shorter of these were published as columns in *The Wind*, Vinalhaven's weekly news and events paper. "Love, etc." was commissioned and published by *The Maine Times*. Nearly all the rest were published by the *Working Waterfront*, a monthly publication of the Island Institute in Rockland, Maine, for whom I write a bimonthly column, and one of those, "Away Happens," was also published by *Yankee* magazine. The essays describe or address events and circumstances occurring in or around my own life on Vinalhaven during a typical year, beginning in the fall.

My wife and I are innkeepers. We own the Tidewater Motel. Elaine is an artist and runs the New Era Gallery right across the street. I'm also a builder.

When an islander dies, whether a year-round or seasonal resident, a basket containing a scrap of paper with the name of the deceased is placed on the counter at Carlene's Paper Store. The exhibit, even if the deceased was well heeled, cues patrons to make contributions of cash, each signing the slip of paper, until quite a sum has accumulated. When a baby is born to an islander, an announcement appears on the window of Bob's hardware store and a flag is flown announcing the birth and the gender. The presence of the basket or the flag is how most of us keep abreast of comings and goings.

The ferry is often referred to as "the boat"; the 7:00 A.M.

boat as the "first" or "early" boat; the late afternoon ferry as the "last" or "late" boat.

It is important that you know these things.

September 2004   P.C.

GLOSSARY

Bait Bag: A small nylon net into which is stuffed bait, usually herring. The bag is then suspended in a trap to attract lobsters.

Davit: A hydraulic device for hauling traps.

Gear: Lobster traps, rope, buoys, and related equipment.

Gurry: Unappealing fish parts, guts.

Out to Haul: Aboard a lobster fishing boat and about the business of harvesting lobsters, hauling traps.

Phil n the Blanks: An acappella singing group comprised of four men, one of whom is me.

Pot Heads: Cone-shaped nets installed at the entrance to and within traps to keep captured lobsters confined.

Pot Warp: Rope used in lobstering, usually the one that connects the trap on the ocean bottom with the buoy on the surface.

Quarry: A deep hole, sometimes several acres wide, where granite had once been mined, now filled with cool spring water and often used for swimming in the summer and skating in the winter.

Roller: A wooden rectangular container built of lathes spaced apart and used for collecting harvested clams.

Seinin' (Seining): Fishing with a large net, floating on the top, weighted on the bottom.

Skidder: A large powerful tractor used to haul logs from the woods.

Washboard: A reenforced portion of the gunwale where lobster traps and gear are hauled aboard

AWAY HAPPENS

An Island Morning

This is a lobster-fishing community, so the process of our familiarity with one another begins before daybreak on any given day—a day in November, for example, after an early snowstorm.

Ralph walks by the house with his dog and glances in, expecting to see me at the table. He knows I'm having oatmeal—real oatmeal—brown bread (left over from Saturday's traditional baked bean supper), coffee, and grapefruit. Ralph's been walking by for so many years that he has witnessed all the stages of my breakfast; he knows the menu, knows the sequence of preparation, and knows I'm listening to National Public Radio because during warmer months my window is open. He knows I have an obsessive-compulsive disorder. He knows I know I'm different, but he thinks I don't quite know to what extent. He scuffs his feet a little on the pavement knowing the sound will cue my dog, whom the morning fire is just beginning to thaw out, to come alive with a challenge. He knows his own dog, Rumsfeld, will respond and that the canine exchange will cause me to look up. Mine is the first face he will see today, and his is the first I will encounter, although, absent a little moonlight, I can't see him; I only know he's there. He waves at me and I wave at the blackness and this island day begins.

Ralph walks on. I remember the time his ninety-year-old grandmother stood up at town meeting and encouraged him to persevere in a heated argument over an appropriation to widen the ditch down at Frog Hollow. "That's it; you tell 'em Ralphie deah. You folks should listen to Ralphie," she admonished those assembled. Anyone else would have been embarrassed, but not Ralphie. He belongs to a family of long island standing, and the capacity for embarrassment has been bred out.

A Dodge Ram goes slowly by; it's Hummer, and although he's only scraped a little patch of frost off his windshield, enough to get him to town if he scootches down and peers over the top of the steering wheel, he toots his horn at my illuminated window not really knowing whether I'm there. Giving Ralphie and Rumsfeld a wide berth down by the fountain, Hummer waves out the side window, gets one in return, and resumes a course roughly in the center of the street, a course he maintains until he sees other headlights, whereupon, at a timely juncture, he shifts a little, keeping just to the right of the oncoming lights, assuming that the other driver has cleared his own windshield more thoroughly and can see where he's going. The pattern of headlights becomes clear, and the six ambers on top of the cab, with the second from the right burning like phosphorous through its broken lens, tells Hummer it's Sonny in his Bronco. No need to waste a wave. Can't see one another with the headlights on anyway. Besides, Hummer's reminded that Sonny once falsely accused Hummer's father of having botched a roofing job as a means of securing work for himself. Well, that was a long time ago; still, Hummer gloats a little because, since then, not much has gone right for Sonny, what with booze, diabetes, and his two boys in constant trouble.

Sonny has cleared his own windshield, and he recognizes the Dodge and knows that Hummer's only scratched himself a little hole to see through. He pulls a little to the left, knowing Hummer is using Sonny's own lights to navigate by, to see if he can drive him into the snowbank. He doesn't like him, hasn't since Hummer's wife joined others on the Planning Board in voting down his boy's application for a redemption center in a residential zone. "They come here from away, all of them board members, and they ought to go the hell back," he offered at the time, and his assessment hadn't moderated any in the years since. "As a matter of fact every tree-huggin' do-gooder on every committee in town moved here from somewheres else, someplace where they wasn't in control or couldn't get along; and they come here and took over." Rounding the corner by the fountain, he sees Ralph walking that pitiful excuse for a dog, miserable little fluffy thing wearing that stupid sweater. He was about to give 'em a little jolt when the siren, sounding from down at the fire station, did it for him. Scary at any time, it's particularly jarring before daylight, especially this time of year, lots of wood stoves. Probably just a chimney fire. Sonny wheels the Bronco around and heads for the station.

Chief Carl Anthony is already there, manning the phone. Turns out it's not a fire. Harold Middleton has had some sort of spell and they're going to try and fly him out, get him to the hospital on the mainland. Fifteen or twenty pick-ups, most of the department, head up island to park along the length of the landing strip, illuminating it enough so the little Cessna can land. Carl is worried about Harold, a retired teacher who moved here twenty years ago who, with his wife, Louise, bought a little piece of land, and carved themselves out a little niche in the woods and in the community. Truly humble, they fit in nicely. Behind the scenes, to the extent that sort of thing is possible out here, they have worked to help others, particularly islanders. Carl was such a beneficiary. When his boy got his arm mangled by a wood splitter, travel arrangements to and from and lodging near the Boston hospital for the visiting parents and family were anonymously provided.

Harold is on the gurney in the ambulance with two EMTs attending. Kneeling on one side is Emily, and, in spite of Harold's grim condition, in spite of his grip on her arm, and in spite of the consuming task of monitoring his vitals, she's drawn to the focused expression on the face of Herbie, the thirtyish leader of the volunteer squad who, kneeling on the other side, is continually transmitting Harold's statistics to the mainland hospital. Emily recalls that a few years ago Herbie won nearly $3 million in the state lottery. Always shy, he was quiet about it, and not many mentioned it to him, knowing he'd be uncomfortable having it discussed. After a time he got a new guitar, then a newer secondhand truck, and, after some more time elapsed, he hired a country western band to come out and play for the townspeople, kind of a gesture of appreciation for just living here. But there still was an awful lot of money left, so he'd come to Harold and Louise and asked for help in managing it. The Cessna dips in, accepts the transfer in the glare of headlights in formation, and lurches off with Harold.

Everyone heads back to town, Herbie and Matt and Burke, the latter two in training, to put the ambulance back in the garage, and Emily to go sit with Louise. The sun's up now and there is more activity as they near town. They pass Dottie MacFarland. No one who knows her can encounter Dottie without remarking on her astonishing transformation, and these four do. Ten years ago Dottie, on an infrequent foray, slipped on the ice and broke her ankle. As she weighed nearly four hundred pounds, it was impossible for any number of men to get her on her feet or into a vehicle. The water company's little utility back hoe had to be used to hoist her into the rear of a truck in a jury-rigged sling and then out again at the medical center. This morning she waves brightly as she trots along. She weighs maybe 140. Whatever combination of things she brought to bear on this accomplishment is not common knowledge, but walking certainly was a mainstay. From the moment she was back on her feet she walked at least three times a day. For the first few months it was only for tiny distances, but everyone could see that it was every step she could muster. We all followed her progress, too, seasoning it with encouragement or admiration or, after all we're a reflection of the world, contempt.

Dottie watched the ambulance disappear around the corner by the quarry as she jogged on and thought about Herbie, Matt, Burke, and Emily and how hard they'd worked to make this ambulance service a reality. Emily had been in her class in school and had resented the ease with which Dottie performed athletically and attracted boys. Not long after graduation Dottie passed up an opportunity to go to college, with all sorts of financial aid, to marry Mark Philip. When she realized what a mistake she'd made, she just kind of grew along with her problems. Emily had gone to Colby, begun a career at Bigelow Labs in Bar Harbor, married a fellow biologist, and had two daughters. Suddenly she turned up here with those two little girls in tow, and she never left again. More often than not we know pretty much everything about everyone, but Emily raised those girls in the bosom of her family and this community, and never said boo about the man who'd fathered them. Now the girls are grown and gone, one married, and the other, an extraordinary young woman, is a senior at Vassar. Of course, it wouldn't have been possible if Ben hadn't—well that's enough for now. Tomorrow's Thanksgiving.

⚓ ⚓ ⚓

Let's Call a Turkey a Turkey

Early on Thanksgiving morning I came downstairs to put the turkey in the oven. Elaine had asked me to do this, she having spent most of the previous day, while I was out carpentering, getting things ready, making pies, and so forth. She said she'd leave me instructions. On the counter was a note. "Sweetie Pie," it began. Notes containing directions for me from her always begin with "Sweetie Pie." It's kind of a softening agent. This one continued: "Pre-heat the oven to 350. Rinse the turkey well, inside and out, with cold water, and pat dry thoroughly. Carefully put the stuffing in the bird; don't cram it. Place the turkey in the roasting pan, breast side up. Rub it liberally with olive oil and this packet of herbs and put it in the oven."

I do enjoy comprehensive directions and settle comfortably into a task so well defined that the absence of even a passing familiarity is no obstacle. I turned on Public Radio, filled the kettle and set it on the stove, and set the oven on "bake" at 350°F. I discovered by myself that the turkey was in the refrigerator and suppressed some minor irritation at her less-than-optimum specificity in not having made the bird's location clear in the instructions. At over twenty-five pounds it more than filled the sink basin, and I concluded right away that the bathtub would be a much easier place in which to accomplish the task of "rinsing well inside and out and drying thoroughly." On my way to the bathroom, cradling the bird to my undershirt, I chuckled at the ever-mounting evidence of how easily a woman's work can be made more efficient by the application of a man's natural capacity for problem solving. I put the turkey in the tub, reflecting all the while on how much more sense this would have made if, when in the shower myself a few minutes earlier, I had simply washed us both. I made a note to streamline this process next Thanksgiving, not only this, my own substantive stage of Thanksgiving dinner preparation, but also my wife's subsidiary work the day before. Doubtless I could save her a lot of time, time during which she might find other useful things to do.

As expected, the tub was the perfect place and the massage showerhead, fitting each cavity perfectly and set on *Stimulating*, brought clarity to "rinse well inside and out." I quickly discovered that paper towels, wet and dissolving in pieces inside the bird, were not the ideal thing with which to "dry thoroughly," but a hand towel, the one I'd used earlier while shaving, worked perfectly.

Back in the kitchen with a squeaky-clean bird I fixed myself a cup of coffee. I love this time of day—early morning, not yet light, that first cup, insightful and timely broadcast news and analysis, being alone and engaged simultaneously in critical food preparation and consideration of the world's difficulties.

I focused once more on the turkey. It had two holes; doubtless some among you already know that. Nonetheless, I'm sure you can appreciate that, given my unfamiliarity and my well-founded assumption that the "instructions" to Sweetie Pie were less than thorough, I was cautious. A large hole was apparent in one end and a smaller opening at the other. It occurred to me that it was not obvious which was the front and which the back. Just as quickly, though, I realized that it didn't matter either, for the instructions said nothing about installing the turkey frontwards. I put the question out of my mind. I did wonder, however, if the small hole at one end was a continuation of the opposite larger hole, whether I could expect the stuffing pushed in to one end to eventually emerge from the other. If so, I reasoned, I'd close up the small end somehow and work from the larger orifice, into which I could more readily fit my fistful of stuffing. With a spelunker's curiosity, I turned off the lights (it was still pre-dawn) and stuck a flashlight in one end. No corresponding illumination could be seen at the other, and neither did the reverse process produce any results other than to lead me to conclude that I would have to stuff both ends separately, and this I accomplished, as directed, without cramming. Still, the bird was quite full, at both ends, full enough that the little flap at the small end would not stay closed and the legs at the other would not stay together. I skewered the small end-flap closed with a lobster pick and remembered from long ago that the legs of my mother's roasted turkeys had been tied together with string, and that this roasted cordage was removed from the small ends of the drumsticks before the bird was placed on the table. I searched around for some string, but wondered before I'd concluded my search if perhaps a special string was required, one that wouldn't ignite in the oven—asbestos string maybe. Unsure, I had the urge to go upstairs and deliver a withering assessment of my wife's woefully incomplete instructions. "These are akin," I was prepared to argue, "to my leaving a note for you that said, 'Sweetie Pie, finish building this wall by nailing each stud as required,' without even explaining to you what a stud is and how would you know otherwise, having never encountered one." Not sure that was exactly the message I wanted to deliver, I stifled the impulse.

A length of something that looked like tendon protruded from the end of each drumstick and seemed to be fashioned into a kind of loop. I concluded that this had been some sort of barbaric hobble visited on the unfortunate bird back at the aviary. One thing was certain; tendons are not appetizing, and these were particularly unsightly. I set about their removal, but a knife wouldn't touch them. Though impressed with its sinewy resistance, I was no less determined. Retrieving a pair of aviation snips from the cellar, my eyes fell upon my orderly assortment of galvanized fasteners, and there, in the form of a three-inch deck screw and a cordless drill, I perceived a solution to the vexing problem of keeping the bird's legs together. Buoyed by my resourcefulness, I hastened back to the problem bird, made short work of the tendons with the snips, and screwed the troublesome legs together with the deck screw.

Nestling the bird in the barely adequate roasting pan, I covered it liberally with olive oil, lubricating every inch, every gentle fold, each appealing crease, every nook, and, in particular, the crannies, and enjoying myself altogether too much. I rubbed in the assembled aromatic packet of herbs and while admiring my handiwork reviewed the instructions. "*Breast side up*" leapt out at me. I turned to look more carefully at the bird.

There was a time, I think not long ago, when an invitation to place a thing "breast side up" would have been one to which I'd have responded flawlessly, with enthusiasm and no small degree of confidence. Now I was confused. I held the bird's tiny wings out to the left and right and tried to imagine it high-stepping around, upright, in the barnyard. Whether a turkey is breast-side-up is not as readily apparent, I observed, as might be the case given a more familiar species. I worried. A labor of love, a response to a note that begins as appealingly as "Sweetie Pie," can sour if it ends with a failure to have followed instructions—instructions whose composition is judged by the person responsible for having crafted them as comprehensive and thorough—a failure like an upside down turkey.

I reasoned that I would have to get the thing out of the pan to be sure. There having been only two ways to put it in the pan, other than by standing it on its head, whichever end that was, I knew there was at least as good a chance I had installed it breast-side-up as breast-side-down, but a fifty-fifty chance wasn't good enough. The prospect of Elaine opening the oven door and wondering aloud if I could not do anything right, perhaps even making a reference to breasts, perhaps with others by then in attendance, loomed large.

Twenty-five pounds is a lot to hold aloft by those tiny, well-oiled wings. Had it not been for the rough texture of the applied herbs I'd have had no purchase at all. Held at arm's length, the legs, screwed together and sticking straight out, offered no clue as to which direction was up. I stuck two shish kebab skewers in the surface that, at the moment, was up, as imaginary legs, and grabbed the wings in such a way that the bird articulated with its new legs pointed downward. Holding on hard to the slippery little wings, I struggled to hold the big bird aloft while trying to imagine it strutting about the barnyard unhobbled, breasts correctly aligned, on its stainless steel prostheses. Basil and oregano are ineffective aggregates. I was relying on the rosemary and thyme to keep the bird in my grasp, and it worked—for a few seconds.

When the turkey hit the floor it landed on its new feet next to the cat which, such acrobatics being its second nature, was unimpressed. The steel legs buckled as the skewers punctured the linoleum, the points at which each bend occurred becoming, effectively, knees. I retained a measure of control and, managing to keep it from falling over, was able to ascertain that the bird was in fact upside-down, that the position in which I had placed the bird in the pan had, indeed, been breast-side-up. I had been, not unexpectedly, right all along.

Elaine came down a little later. She eyed the skewers still sticking out of the linoleum, around which had spread a significant little oil slick. This was to be my visual aid as I delivered a mild rebuke concerning the need, henceforth, for more thorough instructions. The cordless drill and snips were on the counter, and I was graciously prepared to make her a gift of these after having explained their culinary usefulness and having offered other helpful hints intended to improve her performance and efficiency in the kitchen.

As I write, I am down here in the cellar with my dog and the drill and the snips and my orderly assortment of fasteners and have been advised that I can come up again around noon.

⚓ ⚓ ⚓

Dog Town

January 15 was cold and it was blowing hard. I drove down over the hill and into town, nearly paused at the stop sign, and turned left. I'd just shifted into second when, glancing at the bank, I saw its door open and Linda emerge.

Out here on the islands we all know one another, and from this fundamental difference between life for us here and life for others elsewhere evolve other distinctions. For example, since everyone is an acquaintance, as soon as any one of them comes into view the mind hurries instinctively to its own video library and pulls up everything it can remember about that person. Invariably that's more than the subject would prefer and often more than the viewer would like to know. Nonetheless the videos run, automatically and instinctively, like breathing.

And so the Linda video cues up. Linda works at the bank and has for a long time. She knows everything about it. When a manager retired some years ago Linda was jokingly referred to at his retirement dinner as the person solely responsible for allowing that manager, and others, to hang on as long as they did. Like so many other island businesses, the actual names of which are often subordinate to the given name of the proprietor, the bank is regarded and referred to by many as Linda's, as in "I got to go down to Linda's and get some quarters for Bingo."

Volumes more about Linda scrolled down a remote section of my consciousness before it became clear that she was standing out there in the icy cold, on the bank steps, without any coat, waving frantically and hailing me by name. My mind hit the pause button and I thought, "I must have bounced an awfully big check to warrant this sort of attention." In the few seconds it took me to stop I thought it more likely there was some emergency inside the bank. By the time I got out of the van she was halfway across the street running toward me, and I concluded that someone inside the bank was ill and she had hailed me because I was the first person she saw.

"Has anyone talked to you?" she asked.

Loath to pass up any opportunity, I joked, "Well yes, there was that time a few years back," but her continued distress made it clear to me that something had happened to someone in my family and she was trying to determine if I was already aware of it. I was not. I thought of my grandmother, in her nineties and living alone in an apartment north of the bank, of my parents in their home across the street and just south of the bank, of my daughters, Katie and Sarah, at school three hundred miles southeast of the bank, and of my artist wife, Elaine, at her studio at Sand's Cove a mile west of the bank.

"Danny called from the car phone," Linda went on.

Of its own accord Linda's video pops out and the Danny tape pops in. During the winter he works in the woods with his brother and father, Addisons Jr. and Sr., all lobster-men during the season. The three of them are the truest of islanders. Generations of Ameses have occupied the Granite Island neighborhood for so long that even the granite acknowledges their seniority. At one point the video shows Danny sneaking into a neighbor's chicken coop to put hard-boiled eggs under sitting hens.

Linda interrupts the viewing: "A tree fell on your dog. We don't know how he is."

I'm reminded that Linnell took the dog this morning, and the Danny video, accommodating, ejects in favor of hers. Linnell lives at the end of our street with her twelve-year-old son and a cat. She's a gifted landscape gardener with a degree in math from Smith. Her eighteen-year-old daughter, now away at college, is one of my daughter's close friends. Linnell is an alto in a six-person singing group and a frequent dinner guest. She and the three Ames boys constitute Ames Brothers Forest Service. Very blonde, nearly translucent, she and they crammed into the cab of Addison's truck are a stunning and unlikely spectacle; Mia Farrow abducted by Green Mountain Boys, perhaps. Linnell loves my dog, as do the Ameses, and they take him to work with them as often as circumstances permit.

Linda continued, "Rob's on the phone trying to reach Martha." Out comes the Linnell video to join the others, barely sampled, piling up on my mind's floor, and in goes Rob's.

Rob is the bank manager. He and Sandy moved here only a few years ago and brought with them an infectious good humor, happily mingled a little with exhaustion of late. They just had their first child, a girl, over ten pounds. The video reveals they'd been trying for a long time, which may account for their sustained good humor, and that they are the keepers of the coop wherein were found hens laying hard-boiled eggs.

The Rob and Sandy cassette is ejected and the Martha clip begins. Martha is a former vet's assistant and is the first person called in emergencies involving animals. She runs a pet supply and gardening store called Over the Fence and a dog obedience class. She and her husband have a ten-year-old daughter for whom my own Katie happily baby-sits now and then.

The dog is named Yitzhak, ten years old and a hundred pounds. He was named after Yitzhak Rabin, who was Israel's secretary of defense during the late sixties and, more recently, prime minister. I was there during the Six Day War and was so impressed with him that the idea took seed that I would name something of my own in his honor. I made a semiconscious vow to name a son Yitzhak, but we had a daughter so I named my dog instead. Katie is relieved, knowing how close she came. Yitzhak is mistaken by nearly everyone, even vets, as a black lab. In fact his mother was a full-blooded black and tan coon hound and his father was purported to have been a golden retriever. You have to look pretty far down his throat to see any evidence of a golden; I suspect a lab lived in the neighborhood. We got him for Katie, but after we picked him up on the mainland, Elaine drove and I held him during the ferry ride out to Vinalhaven. When we got home I tried to present him to Katie, but by then he had wet himself and whatnot in my lap, and in dog parlance there is apparently no greater reciprocal evidence of devotion than to, on the one hand, bestow such deposits and, on the other, to allow them to be deposited. We'd bonded. I was Mom. Not long after that he began riding in the truck or van and grew accustomed to being let out when we arrived at the dirt road leading to whatever building project I was working on. Several of these roads were at least a mile long. One was two miles. Yitz learned the location of these roads and anticipated disem*bark*ing with great eagerness. Having thus run at least a couple of miles, and often more, nearly every day of his life has left him, now ten years old, in great shape. A few years ago he showed evidence of problems with his hindquarters. At someone's suggestion I began giving him an aspirin and a yeast/garlic tablet each morning. He made a great recovery, and now, though slow to get to his feet and with a gray muzzle, he still anticipates the arrival of a dirt road and the run that follows.

Linda continued, "We couldn't reach you or Elaine so we called your father and he's gone to find one of you."

She told me where the Ames Brothers were working, and I hurried off to Over the Fence. On the way I met my father and, right behind him, Elaine, he having found her. She and I discussed for a moment the best course of action and decided that I would go to the scene but she would remain in town. (Apparently neither my dad nor Elaine maintains a video in my library, because neither of them popped up. I think they may be in the book section.) When I arrived at Over the Fence, Martha, having talked to Rob, was already coming out the door and flipping over a well-worn little sign that now announced to incoming customers "Gone on

Emergency." I grabbed a couple of pet blankets at Martha's instruction and we headed for Calderwood's Neck, seven miles distant. On the way we talked about what we might find. We had no information about where the tree had struck the dog, for example. Trying to ease the apprehension, I observed that with any luck it was his head, where there was very little sense. Unamused, Martha agreed that the head would be best, because there is such a lot of protection (bone) there.

Elaine went home to await word. There was a message from Addison on the answering machine. It was a very sad message, describing how a tree had fallen on the dog and lamenting that it "didn't look good for old 'Yitz.'"

Addison Jr. is the founder of Ames Brothers Forest Service, an occupation he appears to enjoy as much, if not more, than lobstering. He's also president of the Vinalhaven Land Trust and the leader of frequent and popular nature forays following the trust's many trails, most of which have been cleared and maintained by him and other volunteers.

At 10:15 Martha and I arrived at the scene. Smoke was coming from a rise in the woods a hundred yards or so ahead. We could see Addison walking toward us, looking gloomy but not so forlorn that we might readily conclude the dog had expired.

"How's he doing?" we asked simultaneously.

"Well, he's still alive."

"Where did the tree hit him?" Martha asked as she headed off toward the fire.

"Right on top of the head," replied Add. I grabbed the blankets and hurried to catch up.

Up on the bluff Yitzhak, still prone, cradled in Linnell's arms, and fashionably attired in some of her extra winter clothing, heard the familiar sound of my van arriving and of the door opening. Not long before, this dog had very much appeared to have been killed by the falling tree. The imprint left by his face having been driven into the ground was still in evidence; if cast, we'd have had a perfect likeness to hang in the kitchen. He had a hole in the top of his head the size of a tennis ball and couldn't get to his feet. Historically, however, it has been the continual and endless prospect of meeting people, new and old alike, putting his nose in the gathering crotches, and moving them about like pieces on a game board, that has given his life a singularity of purpose. Up over the crest, he could now see, a couple of new players were approaching. He struggled to rise and managed to get his front feet under him. Linnell held him back, fearing he might do himself more damage. Martha reached him first.

I remember when, years ago, a friend of mine ran out into the street to comfort his dog that was lying in the street after being hit by a truck. The dog, his lifelong companion, bit him badly as soon as he reached for it. Nearly broke his heart.

Martha knelt casually in front of Yitzhak, examined his eyes, and then, just as casually, opened his mouth to look at his gums—an indicator, it turns out, of the presence of shock, apparently absent in this case. We turned our attention to the hole in his head, beneath which we could see his skull. It looked like pink granite, and, given the blow he'd received and the recovery he has made since being flown to Rockland and getting sewn up, it may very well have been.

During the next few days Yitz received get-well cards and presents of snacks and chew toys.

Just a dog, some might say. Not out here. Just a life, we are more apt to hear nowadays, but not out here. And winter was just getting started.

⚓ ⚓ ⚓

Spreading Joy

For much of the past decade, we four men, one (myself) tall and youthful, three otherwise, who are the a capella group Phil n The Blanks, have, by generously sharing our gifts, enriched the lives of this deprived indigenous population and have occasionally brought a measure of enlightenment to the lackluster existence of our culturally challenged summer residents too. During this time we have performed at nearly every island venue. Usually we come because we are invited, but, with a mind toward the heavy mantle of social responsibility that comes with being cultural icons, we have nonetheless had to crash the occasional event to which we had not been extended an invitation but whose attendees, we knew, could only profit from our presence. Thus it was that our tenor heard of an upcoming private soiree at which the host had neglected to ask us to perform. This was to be one of those franchised events, in this case, he joyfully reported, a Body Mighty Party, and, while the syntax seemed a little odd, even for auto-repair enthusiasts, we all agreed it must be a rust-proofing workshop. So we rushed through a couple of rehearsals of *Mabeline*, *Hot Rod Lincoln*, and the *Ballad of Thunder Road*, and set out on the appointed evening full of ourselves and of the happy anticipation that comes with knowing one is about to bring joy to others. Unfortunately, or fortunately, depending on your frame of reference, our tenor is, among his other shortcomings, a little deaf, and we found ourselves not at a Body Mighty Party but rather a Naughtie Nightie Party. The lusty nature of the hostess, a fact that had not entirely escaped our attention as we prepared for this gig, now made a little more sense. Still, the ladies were, indeed, appreciative; we each came away with little outfits, and we've been asked to come again next year.

⚓ ⚓ ⚓

Off Season

This was a major nor'easter; forecasters gleefully compared it to the Perfect Storm because of the unusual confluence of a high over the Great Lakes and a low out over the Atlantic and the directions from which, and the energy with which, this whirlwind courtship approached consummation.

Dealing with ferries and the possibility that weather, particularly winter weather such as we were having in such abundance, might adversely affect departures and arrivals is a routine to which we've all adapted. For some, the prospect of inclement weather is so troubling that they might travel to the mainland days, even a week, in advance of a dentist appointment just to avoid the terror of a "bad" boat ride. Others are equally put off by the prospect of needlessly spending the night in a mainland motel and will push the envelope of departure until it looks fairly sure that the weather will permit a return trip. Meteorologists are gleefully referred to, out here on the islands, as alarmists. Their forecasts had become very dire and were accompanied by videos of soaking-wet understudies covered with seaweed and standing next to sea walls among grounded seals and crabs, scenes that reflected conditions moving "downeast," up the coast. As the Perfect Storm drew nearer, some of us, we who had places to go and things to do, began to think, albeit casually, about modifying our travel plans. "Jumpin' Jesus," observed one, employing a colloquialism that would have been stunning were it not for its dulling familiarity, "You'd think it was the end of the world." But it was the news, overheard on the scanner late on Monday, that the Waldoboro Ladies Auxiliary had canceled its Beano that sent us scurrying down to catch the late boat. No videos of half-drowned weatherfolks, no NOAA civil defense alerts, not even Lou McNally urging us to take him seriously could have spoken more forcefully to the extreme nature of impending conditions than did the cancellation of the Waldoboro Beano.

A long and difficult winter sometimes hinders the capacity of a mind, particularly a mind shut away on an ice-bound island in the ocean, to exercise sound judgment. Often such circumstances affect not only the good sense of those not normally possessed of much of it to begin with but also of those who can usually be depended upon to rein them in. The same forces that awaken our physical senses, the great dripping symmetry of island woods under more perfect snow than we've seen in years, seems to dull common sense. This year the whole business kind of nudged some of us round the bend.

Like Rick and Mel. Their daughters, Vicki and Marilyn, sixteen and friends since infancy, were both superachievers who'd never gotten anything but As except when, bolstered by their parents, they allied themselves in a futile effort to add some depth to an elementary-grade reading list and so alienated the teacher that she gave them each a B—allegedly for deportment, but really because she viewed their suggestion as intrusive. Now the girls were juniors and their families were thinking hard about college. And so it was, the cumulative effects of winter and their own tendencies to now and then stray outside the lines being what they were, that Rick and Mel suffered a modest and short-lived lapse of their customary clarity.

Some of us attend an annual midwinter island gathering ostensibly convened to celebrate Robert Burns's life. The thirty-seven brief years of this Scottish poet (1759–1796) gave life, beyond literature, to a popular tradition of assembling on or around his birthday to qualify scotch whiskey and sample the culinary contributions (anything remotely Scottish) of the attendees. Late on that evening this year, after much of the qualifying had been accomplished, Rick and Mel seized upon the notion to pose as a gay couple with two adopted daughters and to travel with them in tow to the admissions office of Harvard University. That stalwart repository of liberal accommodation, they reasoned, would find in such a contemporary and cosmopolitan foursome from an island off the coast of Maine an irresistible call to affirmative action and would fall all over themselves for the privilege of providing financial aid and admission.

This winter affected others of us too, across the board, all ages. Seth and Eric, sixth- and eighth-graders, respectively, went off to the mainland to spend a weekend in February with a couple of brothers (Louis and Rodney Daniels) they'd met during a home game. They took a little money they'd saved up from the summer before. Seth had most of the two hundred dollars he'd made knitting pot heads and repairing traps for his grandfather who still fished a hundred wooden traps out of Dyer's Island. Eric took about the same amount, although he still had quite a bit socked away, having stuffed baitbags most of the summer as a fourth hand aboard his father's boat, the f/v *Sally Ann For Now*. They'd outlined most of their plans with their parents during long interrogations—how they'd go to the movies the first night, seven o'clock show, then home with a pizza. Off to the Snow Bowl on Saturday, at home with movies that night, back on Sunday, second boat. The Daniels' parents would provide transportation and supervision. The Daniels parent—turns out there was only one—had a somewhat more laid-back approach to parenting than either of the island boy's parents. She took them down to Portland and left them at the Poke and Prod, a hair, nail, and body piercing emporium, while she rendezvoused for a few hours with a friend. On the appointed Sunday boat there was no Eric and there was no Seth. There was, however, a boy about Eric's height and build with his distinctive gait but no hair save a tuft of orange in the very center, front, spilling out and forward over his eyes from a hot-pink miniature toilet-tissue tube. The boy appeared to have been shot in the nose, perhaps by Cupid, with a silver arrow whose passage had been interrupted mid-flight by the cartilage between his nostrils. He was accompanied by a boy claiming to be Seth but looking more like a giant Delphinium. He had an odd grimace and a slight speech impediment resulting from a natural tendency to avoid letting his tongue touch his upper palate, at least until the hole anchoring the little gold stud healed up.

They don't call it off-season for nothing, and it's only February.

⚓ ⚓ ⚓

Shades of 2000

§ome may wonder why, following last week's election for selectman, I have not conceded defeat. It's not simply because my loss astonished me, which it did. It's because with each passing day I'm growing more and more skeptical of the results. Why was I not called on election night, as is customary, to inform me of my defeat? Why was I not called first thing the following morning, or why were the results not posted on the Town Office door as they customarily are? These oversights implied to me then and, as whispers of voting and vote counting irregularities grow stronger, imply to me now, that this election was stolen from me, that Bodine's narrow victory and Carlene's significant margin are, at best, suspect.

Consider how many folks in this town, perhaps vote counters among them, are indebted to Bodine for her generosity and kindness over the years. My sources suggest that those folks and their friends and relatives were coerced to vote, that it was made clear they could be easily forgotten if things did not go Bodine's way.

Carlene may have similarly snatched victory from where it might otherwise not have been. Highly placed sources from within her organization report that she and her employees abandoned subtlety in communicating to Paper Store patrons that if the election results were not favorable the time might come when one or another of them, upon death, might not merit the customary basket on the counter, that no donations would be forthcoming, that their passing, their very lives, might go entirely unnoticed.

For these reasons I am, for the moment and while I await the results of an investigation, withholding my concession.

⚓⚓⚓

Love, etc.

On Valentine's Day, my daughter came home in the afternoon, having attended the Mid Coast Health Association's annual prepuberty (referred to by the attendees as Pre-Pooh) class in our school gym. (The actual puberty class would take place a couple of years later.) The speaker, a nurse, had addressed the assembled eight- and nine-year-old boys and girls and was clinically democratic in sharing freely with both groups information that in another time—mine for example—might not have been imparted till later, and which certainly would have been somewhat more targeted. The weighty nature of the material, intimate details of which were dispassionately interjected into the lives of young girls and boys who had heretofore been quite speculative and free-form as they considered one another, was sobering and left my daughter unusually introspective.

Rather than settling in at the kitchen to discuss the events of her day with her mom, as was her custom, she lingered long enough to satisfy herself, through some circumspect questioning, that everything she'd heard was true and that none of it was going to surprise her mother, and then retreated to her room to ruminate and develop a strategy for, or perhaps to decide whether to even bother, bringing her dad, the often uninformed and always unenlightened parent, up to speed. Ever charitable, she decided it was worth a go, and when I came home later in the day, she asked if we could talk. Had we been about to engage over an issue about which we had a disagreement, I'd have been at a clear disadvantage, for she had composed herself and she, composed, is and remains a formidable and furrowed thing.

She seated herself opposite me on the couch and, coming right to the point, asked if I knew that today had been Pre-Pooh Day. As it happens, I did know, and this awareness, not a condition to which I can lay frequent claim nor one to which she has borne frequent witness, seemed to surprise her a little. No matter; our eight years together had left her with a quite firmly held opinion that, while a loving dad, I was largely unaware on many levels, and this business of things biological was likely one of those deficient areas. She apparently felt my role in her own creation had been incidental, perhaps even accidental, but, without question, thought things would have gone more smoothly had I attended Pre-Pooh class.

Fortunately for me, I had her, and she had happily concluded that it was not too late for me to enjoy a measure of enlightenment in the time left to me. Furthermore, those prospects could only improve if, since I was not likely to ever attend Pre-Pooh class, she shared with me some of what she had learned. Given my advanced years, she decided to start kind of at the end, that place where I think she thought I was, with material I might be at least vaguely familiar with, and work backward toward those things about which, if I'd ever known, I had by now likely forgotten. She would educate me first about my wife's body and its current condition and (she would judge as the instruction wore on) perhaps then move on to things regarding the workings of my own body about which I had heretofore remained blissfully unaware.

"Dad, in a few years Mom is going to become a different person. She may become moody and disagreeable and she may cry for no reason and this will be because of changes in her cycle. Are you aware that Mom has a cycle?"

"You're not talking about the one in the garage, are you sweetie?" I offered as a confirmation that we were both on the same page.

"No, Dad, I'm not," she replied, her furrows deepening. "I'm talking about things that happen in a woman's body every month or so during the years when she can be a mom but which then stop happening when she gets older and is supposed to be a grandmother. This thing is called 'the change' because that's what it does. It changes her. A man may experience a change too. It probably won't make him cry but it might make him anxious and peculiar."

"Sweetie, why don't you tell me what you learned today. Some of it may be familiar to me. I know how unlikely that must seem to you, but there also may be some things about which I know nothing. In either event I'm sure I'll benefit if you share it with me and you'll feel better for having done what you can. Start at the beginning."

"OK. When a man and a woman fall in love, like you and Mom did, and sometimes even when they're not in love but are just interested in seeing if they'd like to be, they might touch each other and it's not the same as when a boy on the playground punches me in the arm. Know what I mean?"

"Yes, dear, I do."

"OK, so when you and Mom fell in love some of that happened and I was born. When it started I was just a semicolon."

"You're losing me, sweetie."

"A woman produces an egg every month or so and sends it down to the fallopian tube to see if there are any little visitors. Little visitors are sperm that a man might have put there because of touching. Even though the woman only produces one egg, there are thousands of little visitors trying to get to it. Miss Fricke, she's the nurse, said that a good way to think about an egg being fertilized is to think of a semicolon. The egg is round like the top half of the semicolon and the sperm has a little tail like the lower half, so a semicolon reminds her of a sperm heading upstream to the egg."

"Lets talk more about love. What about love do you understand?"

"Well, I know you love me and I know Mom loves me and I know you love Mom and I know I love both of you and we all love Gram and Gramp and my uncles and aunts and cousins and Emily and Yitzhak [cat and dog]."

"Well, we do say I love you all the time but how do we know when we are really loved or really love someone?"

"I know you love me because you tell me every night when I go to bed and I can just tell you mean it. I know you love Mommy because when I hear a noise from the kitchen that sounds like a very quiet chicken, I know you are hugging her and she is clucking. And I know I love you and Mommy because if anything scares me and I can't get to sleep, noises and stuff, I think about how good it feels to love you both and whatever was bothering me stops.

"Some grown-ups in town, like Betsy at the library, say they love me. She always says 'I love my little hamster.' Rachael at Go Fish doesn't really say I love you but I think she does because she always leans on the counter and her face looks like she is loving someone but she is talking to me. Bob always comes out of the hardware store when I go by and talks to me and when I go he always says 'God loves you' to me but I think he does too. And everybody at the bank does, because when I come in to put money in my savings account one of the ladies always says, 'Who loves this girl?' and then everyone says, 'We do.' And Harold, the bus driver, must love me because he knows my birthday and always remembers it. Those are some of the grown-ups who love me. You know, everybody doesn't have love."

"Like who, sweetie?"

"Well, like Rollie Grogan. He doesn't have a mother, and sometimes when he gets on the bus he looks like he's been in a fight. I think his dad hits him and that's why he is so angry all the time and why he swears and doesn't do his homework. Also, Uncle Ron always comes for Christmas by himself and leaves Aunt Donna at home, so I don't think they love each other. And Fess, the man who sits on the shore behind the post office, doesn't have love. Joey's dog Skidder is always tied up and is definitely not loved, but I can tell he loves Joey because he's all wiggly when Joey comes home, but Joey doesn't love Skidder. He doesn't even look at him."

"What can we do to help them?" I asked.

"We can try to love them anyway. I gave Rollie a Valentine card today before Pre-Pooh class. He didn't say anything but he didn't hit me. I always climb into Uncle Ron's lap and hug him and tell him I love him. I'd like to love Skidder, but he's not friendly to anyone but Joey and might bite. All the third-graders found out when Harold's birthday is and this year we gave him a big card signed by all of us. He had to get off the bus and blow his nose. I don't know what to do about Fess. He's kind of scary."

"What would you like to do?"

"I'd like to give him something like a Valentine card."

"Want me to give it to him with you?"

In a few minutes we were headed down over the hill to town with a big hand-colored and -lettered Valentine card and a bag of heart-shaped cookies from a batch baked earlier. I walked on the outside, she on the inside, her left hand holding my right, her right hand clutching the card and cookies. Fess wasn't at his usual spot, but we found him across the street at the pier, looking out at the fleet. Sarah walked up to him purposefully but didn't let go of my hand.

"Happy Valentine's Day, Mr. Fess," she said and passed him the gifts and then gave him a hug. He hugged her back a little and said, "Thank you, Sarah." He looked at me and then looked at her for a few moments, then he returned his gaze to the sea. We headed back across the street to the sidewalk and back up the hill.

"I didn't know he knew me," she said.

"There are only 1,276 people on this island, sweetie. They've had 3,000 days to get to know you or know about you. Believe me, everyone in your town knows you and cares about you. Many love you. When you're grown up and know them all you'll feel the same."

She was quite buoyed from all this, and when we got home went to the den to make another card. I went into the kitchen to talk with her mom about love and about this extraordinary afternoon. Before long our daughter came in to present us with an enormous card, made from two pieces of cardboard hinged together with yarn.

It read, in big cursive letters, each a separate color: I Love You Both More Than Anyting!!!

She said, "I misspelled 'anything' because the clucking made it hard for me to concentrate."

⚓ ⚓ ⚓

Midlife Crunch

When Lisa settled here a few years ago and opened a health and fitness center, she provided the opportunity and the catalyst for a surprising (to me anyway) population of island women whose latent and earnest desire to improve themselves ran deep. Their numbers grew quickly and the range of participants grew broader. Sorry, bad choice of words. What I meant to say was that the participants were representative of the entire island population of women, from teenagers to ladies in their eighties. There have always been fitness programs, many effective, but this was serious; this was business. Begun in a rented space it shared with others, Island Health and Fitness, several years later and having lasted a few years longer than efforts that have gone before, occupies the top floor of its own handsome building on Main Street, and it is jumping, literally. In the third-floor ballroom where the Knights of Pythias once marched in solemn, secret, and strictly fraternal procession, rows of women now kick, lunge, squat, twist, and, of late, kickbox to compelling, rhythmic musical accompaniment and Lisa's relentless and demanding direction.

Early morning Main Street was once the domain of only a

handful of pedestrians, mostly men: Louie solemnly patrolling, Walt nursing a styrofoam cup of coffee, Ducky waiting for the other Old Duffers to pick him up to go golfing, me setting up the motel to run itself and then heading off to go carpentering, Bobby opening the hardware store, a few pickup trucks whose occupants were loading or unloading (lobster) gear at the town dock, people heading to the early boat, Alvin walking down to the shore. There were virtually no cars on the street or in the parking lot. Now, the ground-level entrance to the big staircase ascending to the third floor of this grand Second Empire Victorian, like a flame attracting moths, accumulates a broad (sorry, sorry again) cross-section of women in leotards and sweat suits for a few minutes every other morning, very attractive shadows of their former selves, who are waiting for Lisa to arrive and open up. Cars not normally seen until later in the day pour into the town parking lot or park on the street; women arriving from closer afield converge here as walkers. And after Lisa arrives, unlocks the place, and they all disappear up the stairs, the effect, dramatic when they were actually there, still lingers. We whose routines have, for years, been solitary—our lives are different because these women are here, first gathered round the door disturbing the peace and quiet, and then, up there, up on the third floor . . . working out.

A surreptitious visit by me early on in the program's development found dumbbells arranged in order in the corner. Little pink one-pounders, like the infants in a family portrait, next to mauve two-pounders, looking up to green apple three-pounders, shouldered to sky-blue fours and fives. Another, more recent, visit reminds me that this is a progressive process. Now the lighter weights, even for new arrivals, are *two*-pounders, and though they're pink, they're electric-pink. Shouldered like soldiers, they stand with green threes and fours, full of themselves next to red fives; businesslike gray eights keep a respectable distance from a pair of cold, black, battle-worthy, take-no-prisoners ten-pound dumbbells: Pam's weights.

The seven o'clock class lasts an hour and then the eight o'clock class begins. These groups, each called Firm Commitment, are the ones Elaine belongs to. For a time, she liked to show me new routines she had learned, usually designed to address the needs of a group of muscles heretofore neglected. Now and then, early on, she actually enticed me to get down on the floor or up against the wall to imitate her newest accomplishment. One such effort involved my getting down on all fours, elevating my head upward as far as I could, and simultaneously lifting my right arm and left leg and extending them to a position parallel to the floor. When I fell over, I struck my right shoulder on the piano stool and my head on an end table and required a good deal of loving care before I fully recovered. On another occasion she had me backed up against the wall trying to coordinate my muscles and breathing in such a way as to force the small of my back flat to the wall while simultaneously touching my left ear with my right foot; at least that's the way I remember it. When that effort produced a minor paralysis, she seemed less inclined to share, quite so personally, her enthusiasm for each successive accomplishment.

Elaine's always been in pretty good shape, has always

taken good care of herself, but in recent years, particularly with the advent of Firm Commitment, she has ratcheted up the effort considerably. Her midlife devotion to being in great shape extends beyond just this very demanding, thrice weekly, hour-long exercise class. She also has taken up swimming in the ocean with a particular enthusiasm for what she refers to as the undeniable feeling that something healthy derives from a return to the primordial soup. And she walks. Our old dog has never been walked very much, not in the formal sense, or had much experience on a leash. Instead he has always been let loose to run alongside the truck once I've left the pavement and headed for one job site or another, and then he's been free to roam around the site all day till we return home—plenty of exercise but no structured regimen. Suddenly, at twelve years old, he's on a leash and accompanying a very focused woman who has decided that a more disciplined approach to exercise will do the dog good.

Some time ago Elaine subscribed to *Walking* magazine and has since looked each issue over carefully. One day last year she remarked enthusiastically on an article she'd found that described a mini-vacation taken by a contributing writer and the writer's companion. It seems there are little yurts in remote scenic areas around the country that are rented by the night to adventurous and hardy vacationers. A yurt is a shelter of material, often canvas, stretched over ribs and set on a wooden platform. Rather more permanent than a tent, it usually is modestly furnished and, in colder climates, may have a wood stove. The writer described, as Elaine read excerpts, waking, stepping out of her yurt, and basking in the brilliant fall panorama afforded by her mountaintop perch in New Hampshire.

The following Christmas one of my gifts to Elaine had been a carefully secured but superficially researched mini-vacation to the same yurt. Naturally irrepressible and impulsive, and thinking it sounded romantic, though, I had scheduled our trip in February instead of enrolling for the moderately comfortable fall excursion described in the article. Elaine managed to convey a barely discernible apprehension as she read the card describing the "gift" and immediately set about finding out everything she could about the proposed trip. She uncovered some details that I might have unearthed myself had I bothered to read any of the material that accompanied my reservation confirmation. For example, it would require a four-and-a-half-mile hike, with a loaded pack, on snowshoes or skis, the last mile or so of which included a near-vertical eight-hundred-foot ascent to our perch four thousand feet above sea level. Tactfully, over the next few days, she began to illuminate the likely rigors of my proposed expedition and, as these weeks after Christmas went by and the time for our departure grew nearer, it became clear, to my astonishment, that it was not herself for whom she was concerned; it was me. Am I not a veteran; have I not refrained from smoking for nearly ten years; can I not, for all intents and purposes, get in and out of my nice new insulated monkey suit all by myself; do I not, with never—hardly ever—more than two or three direct shots of cortisone, recover quickly from a lower back spasm? Does she think that, simply because I have never snowshoed or done much cross-country skiing, because I seem to her a little tired after carrying a twenty-five-pound sack of flour from the store to the car, because I choose to drive the three hundred yards from home to downtown rather than walk, just because I do not have the time to indulge myself in a little loosening-up exercise three times a week, does she think I am not up to carrying a sixty-five-pound backpack up a little hill to our yurt? Well, truth be known, it appears she does, in fact, question my abilities in this regard. I am deeply troubled, of course, but sweetly anticipating the font of respect and renewed admiration in whose glow I expect to flourish for a good long while once our little trek is concluded.

Just to satisfy myself, I have quietly measured four and a half miles here on the island, in my vehicle. It's just the distance from our house here in town up to Jim and Colleen's on the North Haven Road. Not long after, also on the sly, I walked it. Piece of cake. Took me about an hour and a half. Paved road, perfectly flat, temperature around 40°F.

Time and other commitments have derailed our plans to redeem this gift package, but we will, one of these Februarys.

⚓ ⚓ ⚓

Two Strings Attached

We went to Florida in April a few years ago, ready for a somewhat more customary vacation. I'd never seen a woman in a thong bikini before. Of course, I'd seen pictures of them over the years in magazines other guys bought and showed around, but seeing them actually moving around close enough to—well—study, is different. I'm glad I waited. At this stage, happily married and with an adolescent daughter, it was my natural interest in structural engineering and design that was aroused.

The blonde who would before long occupy my first thong bikini showed up around mid-morning in shorts and a tank top and arranged a chaise lounge poolside right next to me. She was beautifully browned and gorgeous. There were other places she could have stationed herself, and so it didn't seem much of a leap to assume that lying there in my blue polyester swim trunks, only hours before on the shelf at Ames in Rockland, she found me tempting. That the novelty of that much male Maine epidermis nearly dead for lack of vitamin D, of a complexion that would have made the Aryan nation proud, in a sea of perfect brown bodies, excited her a little.

She had a small bag and withdrew from it a couple of towels, a pack of cigarettes, a Zippo lighter, sunglasses, and a paperback copy of *Clear and Present Danger* (no, I'm afraid it was lost on me). I rolled over onto my back. I didn't want my varicose veins to frighten her away. An attendant came around immediately and asked her if she'd like anything. (I'd already been there fifteen minutes and he hadn't even spoken to me.) She asked for a Bloody Mary and a bottle of Panama Jack.

"Boy," I thought, "here it is only mid-morning and she's ordering two drinks."

I was the only other person nearby, and so, thinking she was going to introduce herself and offer me one of her drinks, I stretched out to maximize the impact and to minimize my stomach, which had relaxed comfortably around the top of the trunks. I sucked it in and began to time those moments when its features were allowed to settle into their customary positions to coincide with those infrequent moments when she was not admiring me.

Suddenly a young brunette came flying around the corner on roller blades and, groping for some purchase on my chaise, lurched to a stop next to "us" (our relationship had matured in my mind).

"Where's your suit, Hope?" she asked.

Hope held up her Zippo and flicked it open. From within its top she withdrew a little string and some tiny swatches of cloth. It looked like the semaphore flags from *Malibu Barbie*.

"Right here, Vicki. I'll go put it on," said Hope. I gulped audibly and marveled at the foresight of someone twenty-five years ago naming her Hope.

In a few minutes she returned and—there is a God—she was wearing something that had been previously residing, albeit not as happily, in the top of a Zippo lighter. Her companion emerged from the changing room in a similar outfit and arranged herself on a chaise nearby.

The motel routinely posts SUNBURN WARNING next to the pool. It was changed every few hours. Presently it read:

Danger of Sunburn 10 Minutes
Danger of Severe Sunburn 15 Minutes.

The sense of extreme heat on my skin awoke a distant memory reminding me I should roll over, and I did, but before long, already having been on my belly for the prescribed ten minutes before the throngs of thongs arrived, I could feel the sun saying: "You're pushing your luck. Why don't you gather up your things and your urge to procreate, go back into the shade, and join the other men who are making believe they're reading as they admire this duo through their sunglasses."

I rolled over and sat up, allowing my towel to drape itself over my shoulders so that its ends hung down and covered my chest, which rode nowadays so much lower than it used to, side by side, as it were, with its companion ego. The Bloody Mary had arrived by now, and I recognized the Panama Jack for what it was, as Vicki liberally smeared it all over herself. It wasn't a drink for me, and she and Hope had chosen this spot next to me for the angle of the sun. I gazed at that place in the middle of her back she couldn't reach and thought about how useful I could be. Then I began to recognize the tingle I felt for what it was, sunburn, and not the anticipation of my youth. My last words to Elaine before she'd left for her walk down the beach rang in my ears: "Suntan lotion is for sissies."

I stood up, gathered together my vanity, my few belongings, and my excess skin, and headed back into the shade.

Home in Maine we had some friends over for dinner. We spread pictures of our trip all over the table. Karol zeroed in on a clandestine shot Elaine had taken of me preening myself next to the ladies and observed, "Well look. Victoria's Secret meets Modern Maturity."

⚓ ⚓ ⚓

Substitute Driver

She is just a little kid, a first-grader. She has bounced around now in this school bus, every morning and every afternoon, for several months. For a long time she worried about whether she'd get to school in one piece, and then worried all day about whether she'd be returned home safely. Finally, after having ridden with the same driver for a few weeks, her concerns began to subside. And now this.

She gets to the top step, looks toward the driver's seat for the small assurance of seeing his familiar face, and finds instead, under a mop of gray hair, me, an old man, certainly too old to be driving anything, let alone a bus. I'm peering over my glasses and seem unaware not only of her but of pretty much everything else. She searches my face for an indication that there is even the remotest chance I am capable of delivering her home. There is none. Then she glances despondently down at the note in her fist, instructions from her mom that she be delivered to Grammy's, and she realizes that all hope is lost. I don't know who she is or, or perhaps who I am; I certainly don't know who her grammy is. She stalls at the top step, remembering now that I am the same old guy who buried the bus in the ditch over at Indian Creek last fall during my only other substitute appearance. Panicked, she tries to retreat, but there are others piling up behind her, all urged on by the gentle albeit persistent nudge of the teacher on duty. She wants to cry out, "there is a deceased person at the wheel," but no one can be heard on the bus of Babel. Imploringly she passes me the note and I regard it blankly. It might as well have read. *My name is Phil Crossman. I am old and forgetful and will probably lose all of these children.*

To her astonishment I do complete the route safely and deliver each kid to the correct destination, keeping my wits about me just long enough; but apparently no longer, for she hears, as does the whole town, that I later abandoned the bus at the motel with its flashers on, and that during the fifteen minutes or so during which I was blissfully and typically unaware, six westbound cars and twenty-seven eastbound (the ferry having just unloaded) vehicles dutifully piled up behind it waiting for permission to pass. Her mom requests that, if I am going to continue to be a substitute driver, the school please give a little notice so alternative arrangements can be made.

⚓ ⚓ ⚓

It's All in a Name

You'd think with a last name of Roberts that Robert would be a poor choice for a first. And you'd think, too, that Robert Roberts might have chosen a name other than Really for his own boy. But that was it, the boy's name was Really Roberts. The story that went around most, of course, had to do with his father's incessant and doubtful inquiry during gestation and his mother's equally frequent and adamant response. Now and then Really's tormentors would refer to him as Partly or Maybe, and he found that when his full name appeared in print, his fortunes often hung on the placement, within or following Roberts, of an apostrophe or question mark.

Our new transfer station, a decade old or so, has provisions for sorting recyclables and so forth. It also boasts an enclosure called the Swap Shop, and there the thoughtful and frugal among us deposit our cast-off stuff and retrieve things we think might be useful. That's where Flutter Williams found Really Roberts early on a recent Wednesday morning. Really was standing in the entrance to the Swap Shop with his arms wrapped around a very nicely turned-out upright dress form nearly a head taller than he was.

Really's wife, Bottoms, not only thoughtful and frugal but also optimistic, had deposited him at the Swap Shop hours earlier, hopeful, apparently, that someone might find him interesting enough to take home. Bottoms had come by her name not in the way that an over-eager reader may surmise, but because she had, for years before she settled here, been the most aggressive and productive of a crowd of Waldoboro clammers. As soon as she stepped out of the boat, she'd bellow, "Bottoms up!" and then assume that position, flailing away till her roller was filled. Bottoms settled here with her first husband, who was a county deputy. When it developed that he was also an arsonist, Bottoms found herself with some of his official gear, stuff that hadn't been on his person when they took him in, like the arrangement of restraints he'd wishfully brought home with him one night shortly before his apprehension. Thus it was that Really was found standing, or at least on his feet, hugging the aforementioned dress form with his wrists handcuffed together in the small of its back. The mannequin's bust, in turn, had been cranked up, to maybe a 38D, so there was quite a strain on the handcuffs, effectively locking them in an enduring, if less than passionate, embrace.

The dress form had been there at the Swap Shop for some time, the attendants having grown quite fond of her and reluctant to let her go. She appeared daily in a new outfit salvaged from the shop's considerable and continually replenished stock of cast-off clothing. Often this stuff was top-drawer, discarded only because it didn't suit someone's taste or the moment. The crew named her Miss Cleo, memorializing a member of the Board of Selectmen who'd come around far too often issuing opinions about the ways things ought to be done, predicting the failure of systems set in place by others, and generally short-circuiting the chain of command that gave oversight of the Transfer Station to the town manager. This selectperson had, for several years, carried the nickname because of her resemblance to the ill-fated TV clairvoyant. Accordingly, during those first few months, her namesake was dressed in a mocking way and consulted disparagingly whenever a decision had to be made.

Then, too, she would be moved around the site, often outrageously attired, to oversee the comings and goings. After a while, though, she grew on them. Specifically, she grew on Flutter Williams, senior attendant, whose own solitary life was now softened at night by two companionable cats and, during the day, by the equally companionable Miss Cleo. As a boy he had acquired and had since sustained the habit of, when anxious, raising his hands to about shoulder level and waving his fingers or, if particularly stressed, flapping his hands from the wrist. Soon he was being told not to "get all aflutter over it," and it stuck. Over time Flutter had selected, from among the items deposited daily at the Swap Shop, clothing and accessories that he felt complimented Miss Cleo. Washing and ironing and making repairs at home, he kept her wardrobe clean and pressed on a row of hangers and in a chest of drawers in a back corner of the Transfer Station office. For a time he and his activities, which he made sure did not interfere with his duties, were modestly made fun of by his fellow attendants and ridiculed quite harshly by a few local rednecks whose narrow range of understanding could be explained, even forgiven, through only a cursory consideration of their ancestry. Anyway it passed. After a tormented childhood during which his own proclivities were unclear to him, and a less unhappy young adulthood during which those issues became, if not less painful due to the sustained intolerance around him, then at least clearer, and during which time he found, briefly, a romantic interest that suited him, Flutter was now at middle age, gentle and, to his great credit, forgiving. He was alone but accepting of and accepted for who he was; he was content. On this morning, Flutter had driven to work in an ebullient frame of mind.

The previous day, the weather being consistent with approaching spring, Flutter had, after briefly discussing it with her just after closing, dressed Miss Cleo in a smoky-violet fleece turtleneck, stone microsuede cropped pants, and a really sweet cotton velveteen jacket. A turquoise drop necklace and silk scarf completed the ensemble. Flutter wished her a pleasant evening, alluding to an imagined engagement, went home, and retired full of the anticipation that sustained him nowadays, that of returning to work early the next morning to freshen her up a little before the day got started and her public began trickling in and, on this particular occasion, to find out how her evening had gone.

Really was just emerging from the excesses of the night before, just coming to grips, as it were, with his situation, when Flutter pulled back the canvas flap covering the Swap Shop entrance only to discover that the romantic evening he'd imagined for Miss Cleo had come to this wanton end. So distressed was he that Flutter ignored Really's imploring solicitations for assistance and instead left them both there to reflect on their behavior and circumstances.

Around seven o'clock Bait Dyer, junior attendant and equipment operator, showed up. Bait was short for Baitbag, a handle he'd earned on the day after his graduation from high school, when he accepted a bet that he couldn't get himself into a lobster trap and shut the door. In fact, being tiny, wiry, and double-jointed, he'd done it without much trouble. After having removed the potheads and partition from the wooden trap, he'd squirmed in through the door and, from a kind of fetal position, extended one finger from the hand folded upward over his chest and did that which no one before or since has ever done—he closed the trap door, thereby establishing himself and his accomplishment in the annals of island lore. If it had ended there... but of course it didn't. His companions tied the button down and drove through Main Street with the trap on the tailgate, announcing to all that lobstering technology had experienced a great leap forward with the discovery of a better bait than herring, and one that needn't be kept fresh as could be readily seen from this specimen, and they were about to prove it. Then they tossed him up on the washboard of the *Bethany Anne for the Long Haul* with thirty fathom of rope and buoy attached and struck out, about a dozen of them, all pretty well oiled, for the East Side. Bait never went on the water again and has worked at the Transfer Station ever since.

Bait was regarding Really and altogether maintaining a pretty serious countenance, not giving much credit to Really's pleas to be released from bondage, but instead cautioning him against mucklin' onto just any woman in the dead of night and counseling him of the need to be more cautious and discriminating. Just then the first customer, as always Betsy LeFleur, up bright and early and eager to discard a load of asphalt shingles she'd picked up herself to save money after a recent roofing job at her place, started for the demo trailer but stopped first at the Swap Shop to unload a malfunctioning blender. "I'll swap you this for him," she told Bait, "but leave the handcuffs on."

⚓ ⚓ ⚓

Stunted Development

Once, employing the time-honored approach to conflict resolution embraced by a small handful of closely bred islanders, someone busted out all the windows in my prized Volkswagen Camper Van and slashed all its tires. In narrowing down the list of suspects by eliminating those who were not responsible, I determined it was not a woman. At the time, 676 women lived here, and only thirty-four of them were capable of heaving a fifteen-pound boulder with enough force to cause it to pass through the window on one side of the vehicle and out through a window on the other. Of those thirty-four women, six were relatives with whom I was on good terms, eight were Republicans and thus incapable of criminal behavior, five were evangelical Christians and so equally unlikely, six had demonstrated a fondness for me, one worked for me now and then and I didn't owe her any money, and the other eight, while admitting they did not like me, all said they think I'm funny and they wouldn't do such a thing and I believed them.

So it had to be a man, or at least a male with pretensions to manhood. Of the 606 males then in residence, 151 were children and 82 retired, and no one in either group was a candidate. Of the remaining 373, I was close friends with 16, on good terms with 237, casually and pleasantly acquainted with 41, and happily did business with another 74. The remaining five were openly hostile to me. Four would not have resolved their differences with me like this, however. One even said, "I don't wave or speak to you, but if I did I would say I didn't do it." The fifth, the male who had not achieved manhood, was wavering mightily in its pursuit, and was farther from the goal line than when he started, did it.

⚓ ⚓ ⚓

Remote Control

At quarter to one on a Wednesday in May,
a telephone rang at the Half Moon Cafe

in Claremont, New Hampshire.

It wasn't the regular phone, not the one behind the counter, not the one that rang when the cafe's regular number was dialed and that prompted either Kelly or Melissa to answer dispassionately, "Cafe." No, this ringing was coming from booth number three where, an hour before, Elaine, Katie, and I had enjoyed lunch on our way to Massachusetts to look at colleges. By now, however, the booth was occupied by four local businessfolk who lunched here at the Half Moon regularly on Wednesdays and were partial to the turkey reuben with sauerkraut. Brian, owner of the Corner Book Store, was sitting nearest the wall in the booth, which offered a view of the street. After a few rings it dawned on Brian and the rest of the patrons that the ringing seemed to be coming from him.

"Hey, big shot, answer your phone," suggested Roger. Roger owns a machine shop.

"I don't have a cell phone," said Brian defensively. The

phone rang for the fourth time, and he lifted up a copy of the local paper, the *Eagle Record*, left on the seat by an earlier customer—myself as it happens—revealing a Motorola Microtac 650 cell phone just as the thing issued its fifth angry demand for attention. He flipped it open and said, "Hello."

"Got a room?" asked the man's voice on the other end.

"Huh?"

"Got a room for tonight?"

"Huh?"

"I'm down here in the lobby, got a room?"

"Who are you callin'?"

"Damned if I know. This is Jeremy Squires. I stayed here at the motel last night and thought I'd be done work today but I need to stay another night."

"What motel?"

"The Tidewater. Who the hell am I talking to?"

"My name is Brian. I'm just sitting here having lunch and I heard a phone ringing. I found it under a pile of newspapers and answered it."

"Sitting where having lunch?"

"I'm here at the Half Moon Cafe."

"Where the hell is the Half Moon Cafe?"

"Why, it's down here to Claremont."

"Where the hell is Claremont?"

"New Hampshire. Where are you?"

"Vinalhaven, Maine. I just come into the lobby here at the motel and, as usual, there's nobody around, but there's a note on the counter that says the owners are traveling and if I want something to call this number."

"Well, they must of been here and left their phone," said Brian. "Hold on a minute." He turned to his companions to explain but Rick interrupted him. Rick is a contractor, but years before he and his wife had run a small motel over in Hanover. "We heard him, Brian," said Rick, "Ask him does he still have his key from last night?"

Squires heard him. "No, but I know where they keep 'em, right here in this little drawer."

"Then tell him to find a room that's empty and help himself. A place in Maine ain't full in the middle of March now, I'll bet. Tell him we'll hold."

After a minute Squires came back on the line to report that he'd found an empty room.

"Well I guess it's yours."

"And don't forget to fill out a registration card and leave it on the counter so they'll find it when they get back, whoever they are," reminded Rick.

"How does he pay?" Brian asked the others.

"I heard that," said Squires. "Well, this is ain't unusual for this place. Half the time there ain't nobody around. I'll write out a check and tack it to the door to Hair Haven. That's what most of us do."

"What's Hair Haven?" asked Kathy, her interest piqued.

"It's the hairdresser's salon right off the lobby."

"Not bad," acknowledged Kathy, who kept track of the great range of names for hairdressers she'd seen in her own travels. So far she liked Scissor Excitement pretty well; that'd been up around Bangor. Hair's Looking at You wasn't bad either; she'd seen that up in St. Johnsbury; but the best had been Curl Up and Die, which she'd seen one spring when she and her husband, at an American Legion Beano, won a week at a B&B in Llandudno, Scotland. Her own Groomingdales was right across the street from the Half Moon.

"Well, if you know how much it's going to be go ahead and leave the check. Which room are you taking? The owners may call here once they realize they've left their phone. If we're still here we'll need to tell 'em what's going on."

"I'm taking number 7," said Squires.

"OK. Bye now." Brian hung up.

Maria came over with their sandwiches, and Brian began to explain to her about the phone and how they'd answered it and how they figured the owners would be back for it before long or call asking about it. Just then it rang again and Brian answered again. It was Squires again. "Someone else is here looking for a room."

"Well who are they? Are they regulars like you?"

"Oh yeah. It's the substitute bank manager. She has to stay another night 'cause the late boat ain't goin'."

"What's a boat got to do with anything? What happened to the regular bank manager?"

"Well, I guess you wouldn't know but this is an island. We're twelve miles offshore and it's blowin' a wicked breeze out here today and the boat ain't runnin'. This woman come over from the mother bank on the mainland to fill in for Rob who was on vacation and she was going home today but now she's got to stay another night. Probably there'll be others needin' a place too, since the boat ain't runnin'. Lot of people come over here for business and go back on the last boat."

"Well, what other rooms are available? How many rooms does this place have anyway?"

"Oh a dozen or so I'd say. There's five or six cars in the parking lot, but that's all the parking they have anyway. If you want to hold on I'll go take a good look. Usually if the curtains are drawn, not that they cover all that well, that means there's someone in there. If they're open, even a little, you can usually peek in."

"OK. We'll wait."

While Squires was conducting his inventory, the diners talked over their responsibilities relative to the motel and the predicament of their fellow small businessfolk, traveling somewhere here in northern New England, perhaps even heading back to the cafe to retrieve their phone. What with the boat not running and the likelihood of more business, they decided that if the motel owners hadn't returned by the time they were through with lunch they'd stay there in the cafe one at a time and tend the phone in shifts.

Squires was back. "Looks like they got four vacancies and one that's questionable. I took the master key with me; they keep it right here on a nail. The curtains was drawn on one room, enough so I couldn't see in but not so far that it looked like anyone really wanted their privacy, but when I got the door open a little way I heard a woman sound a little note of alarm so that one's probably out. I'd say four for sure."

"Which numbers are they? We've got to keep track of this."

"Well, I got 7 like I told you. I'll give Petria here number 8. The motel will just bill the bank directly for her so you don't have to worry about that. That leaves numbers 3, 4, 6, and 10."

"OK. Thanks, and thanks for staying with us here at the Backwater," replied Brian.

"Say, you're settling into this hospitality business pretty naturally," commended Rick after Brian had hung up. "However, although I can't remember the name of the place I doubt it was the Backwater."

"It was something with "water" in it," said Kathy.

"How about Graywater?" suggested Roger.

Just then the phone rang. Rick answered. "Thanks for calling the Make Water. Can I help you?"

⚓ ⚓ ⚓

Ferry Rules

There are two ways to get your car or truck off the island. One, sanctioned by the Maine State Ferry Service (MSFS) but complicated, is to put it on the ferry. If you choose this method you need to learn the rules.

TICKETS

First, You need a ticket.

1. A $16 round-trip ticket purchased in VH can be used to get you off the island and back.

2. A $30 round-trip ticket purchased in Rockland can get you to the island and back.

3. A $16 round-trip ticket purchased on VH cannot be used to get you from Rockland to VH and back.

4. A $30 round-trip ticket purchased in Rockland can be used to get you from VH to Rockland and back.

5. If a round-trip ticket is ripped in half by an unauthorized ripper it will be confiscated. If the ticket has been or is rumored to have been in your mouth or in the mouth of an acquaintance it will be confiscated by a designated MSFS Hazardous Material employee wearing protective clothing.

RESERVATIONS

If you want to get your car off the island thirty days hence you can come to the terminal and sign the clipboard. After the next person comes you can go home. You must then return at 7A.M. to prove you are the person who signed the clipboard.

If you want to get your car off the island the next day you can come to the terminal, but there is no clipboard so you can't go home; you must stay there and keep track of yourselves and of the order in which you arrived. You must also gauge whether it is worth hanging around, since there is no way of knowing whether you'll actually secure passage until the terminal opens and heretofore unavailable information about what sort of priority traffic is already in front of you is released. This applies only to the first two boats.

The other way to get your car off the island is to drive it overboard, which is less complicated and often more satisfying.

⚓ ⚓ ⚓

Speedy Delivery

There is a long history and, given the logistical difficulties that go hand in hand with remote island living, an easily understood tradition of finding alternatives to conventional methods of delivery. Folks who have a need to get stuff on or off the island routinely swing down by the terminal to see if they can find someone willing to take it one way or the other. Likewise, we who are eager to have something sent over are likely to direct the cooperative mainland merchant to the terminal for the same purpose: to find a vehicle coming this way. Islanders do a lot of business with florists, nurturing new romances, restoring old ones, communicating condolences or congratulations. Flowers are commonly sent along in such a fashion.

Once a year the Lions Club hosts Ladies' Night at the restaurant, and it's customary to present each woman who attends with a rose or carnation. This year, on the fourth Thursday in May, a Rockland florist dutifully sent over a couple of orders on the last boat. Club member Larry went down to retrieve the club's assortment. Sure enough, there in the back of a '92 black Ford half-ton, along with a muffler for the garage, a package for the boatyard, a bundle of *Bangor Daily*s for the Paper Store that had been misrouted earlier in the day, and all the mainland purchases of several walk-on passengers who had more than they could carry, were two unmistakable long white cardboard boxes wrapped in both directions in blue ribbon. Before the truck had even come to a stop, Travis MacDonald emerged from the shadows, darted in among the other consignees, plucked one of the two flower boxes from the truck bed, and disappeared. The driver got out to explain to Larry that the tags had blown off the boxes during the ride across and when he'd reattached them he wasn't sure the right tags were still on the right boxes. "I'd liked to have told Travis but he was off quicker than gullshit through a tin whistle. I 'spect he was takin' them flowers somewheres they ain't s'posed to go."

Well, flowers was flowers as far as Larry was concerned; he grabbed the remaining box and returned upstreet to the restaurant. He was stumped for a moment, when he opened it, to find a broad range of blossoms and greenery instead of the several dozen roses or carnations he'd always distributed in the past. He tried to share his puzzlement with the others assembled, but there was such a hubbub, it being happy hour and all, that nobody paid much attention, and so he dutifully passed them out. There *were* two nice red roses, and he gave one to Dottie and the other to Francis, the club's customary cooks and regular guests of honor. The other spouses and girlfriends received freesia, mums, carnations, lilies, daisies, iris, liatris, and asters. As it happened, there were just about enough to go around. Joannie MacDonald was the last recipient, and Larry ceremoniously presented her with all that remained—two delphiniums and the bunch of gypsophila and ferns that had served as a backdrop and to which was attached, unnoticed by Larry, a card which read "Lil, Thanks for the Memories," and was signed "Love, Travis," a revelation quickly shared with those gathered and that provided more than enough fodder for the rest of the evening.

Don Patterson, the UPS driver, long known as Dontheoopsman, usually distributes most of his load right on the ferry. If he doesn't see the addressee personally, he'll find a relative or an acquaintance upon whom he can unload responsibility for the package. By the time he leaves the boat his truck is almost empty, and he employs the same resourcefulness and economy of effort in delivering the few that remain. Once he left a package for Ira Flecker at the home of Beetle Williams, because he knew, as did everyone else, that Ira was seeing Beetles' wife, Yvonne, and that he'd be by that evening cause Beetle was out seinin'. After a while Don started leaving packages at the island's only gas station because he knew that, eventually, everyone fuels up and would thus sooner or later get their packages. The gas station attendant, a cousin, proved cooperative, taking inside each night those packages that were not picked up, so the weather didn't get the best of them.

Deputy Duffy McFadden set a speed trap up toward Granite Island, tucking his Jeep cruiser in behind a particularly abundant forsythia and a big blue lilac, both flourishing in the soggy ground downhill from Billy Waynwright's woefully inadequate leach field. Billy had installed, nearly overnight, an enormous modular on the lot left him when his grandfather died. The old man had lived there, frugally and alone, for nearly half a century, in his little two-room cottage with the cold-water tap. A flush toilet had been comfortably served by the old cesspool, laid up in paving blocks back in the twenties. Billy had the little house torn down and, because the issuance of plumbing permits and, in turn, building permits, is dependent on, among other things, the number of anticipated bedrooms, he cleverly claimed that the new modular had three dens but only one bedroom, the two full bathrooms notwithstanding, and was permitted to hook into the cesspool. Then he and Sadie Sullivan moved in with her two kids plus two of their own. Of course each kid had his and her own den. The old cesspool was a little overwhelmed. But that's neither here nor there.

From a particular spot in among the foliage Deputy Duff had an unimpeded view of traffic coming and going but, having practiced several times late at night during the preceding week, he knew he could exit quickly if necessary. During those practice sessions he'd squirreled himself away under the bushes, clocked the infrequent motorist with his radar gun, and, after the unwary traveler was out of sight, executed a speedy exit in imaginary hot pursuit. One night he'd clocked Wesley Arsenault heading back home from Cap'n Merrithew's. Wes was doing a steady twenty-six miles per hour. Duffy knew he was a under the influence but Wes always drove at about this pace as if to compensate for his reliably unsteady condition. He wasn't the threat Duff was looking for. He was looking to nab Bo Simpson or Ethan Philbrook or Liam MacDonald or maybe even the cagey and evasive Pumpkin Stockwell. Pumpkin was sternin' for Eaglebeak Bunker out to Matinicus, but lobsterin' still hadn't picked up, this being a pretty bleak spring, and Pumpkin could be counted on to turn up back here on this island once or twice a week. He'd been back home for a night four days before and raised all kinds of hell. Duffy was certain he'd be back on this night, it being Friday.

Duff backed the blue Jeep into his hiding spot during a lull in the traffic around 3:30 P.M. and settled in. If Pumpkin came back from Matinicus today, probably pretty well lit by the time he got here, he'd leave his boat on the mooring at Old Harbor, jump in his truck, and "book it" into town. Pumpkin had been a real nemisis for as long as Duffy had been the Knox County deputy in residence, about a year; he'd nearly had him a couple of times and now he was chafin'.

Duff had been sequestered there nearly an hour and, in the heady aroma of the lilac in flower, had nearly dozed off a couple of times. Around 4:20 he saw the UPS truck heading back toward town. It started to brake as it approached his speed trap and stopped inexplicably at the very spot where Duff had intended to execute the aforementioned speedy exit if called for. To his astonishment, Dontheoopsman dismounted and began walking directly toward Duff's hiding place. Duff was thinking maybe Don was going to relieve himself there in the bushes and how silly they'd both feel when he realized the deputy was hiding in there, but no, Don ducked under an overhanging branch and came right up to Duffy's window, carrying a small package. "Duff," said Don, "I only got this one package left. It's for Pun'kin Stockwell. I just seen him tying up to his mooring but I ain't got time to wait for him 'cause I gotta make the late boat. The guys up island all said you was hauled up here in the bushes waiting to nail Pun'kin. Maybe you could give him this package same time you give him a summons. Thanks, Duff, I owe ya one." He shoved the package through Duff's open window and was gone.

It kind of took the wind out of Duffy's sails to find his carefully crafted and presumably camouflaged speed trap regarded so casually. While he was mulling over his options, trying to decide whether to stay put and risk the ridicule that would come from finding that his speed trap was common knowledge, or to squeeze a little farther back into the brush in the rapidly diminishing hope that an unsuspecting Pumpkin would come by, the subject himself appeared around the corner and nosed right into Duff's hiding place. "Duff," he said, "the guys told me they sent Don down to you with a package for me."

Duff gave it to him, and Pumpkin thanked him, told him to have a nice day, and allowed as how living in a small town is great.

⚓⚓⚓

Old Duffers

Golf doesn't interest me, but if it did I would credit the example set by Ollie, Woody, Bud, and Ducky—all octogenarians. Ollie is remarkably agile, with the flexibility and appearance of well-chewed beef jerky, gummed but not swallowed. Woody recently underwent a serious knee operation. His companions are suspicious of his motives, worried that he might now enjoy an unnatural advantage out on the links. Ducky, at eighty-two, recently enjoyed nationwide exposure when the Associated Press, having done a piece on island voter registration, plastered the nation's papers with a picture of him on election day reading his ballot with a magnifying glass. Bud, also at eighty-two, is so far unhampered by infirmities. A somewhat younger Paul, not long ago, apprenticed himself to the foursome. He'd had a knee operation that left him hobbling along with one leg several inches shorter than the other. The handicap made him a palatable companion; a man in better shape wouldn't have been taken under their wings.

When God thought up this game these are the guys he had in mind: real golfers. They gather three times a week down at Vinalhaven for breakfast and then head up island

and climb into a small outboard for the ride across the Fox Islands Thorofare to North Haven where there's a nice nine-hole course. Rain, or the likelihood of it, does not stop them. If it's not raining now, it never will. If it is raining now, they surmise, it may not be by the time they get to the first hole. If it lets up for even a moment it is "showing signs of clearing." One year, with an open January and a little warm spell around the end of February, they made it up at least once in every month of the year. That's quite an accomplishment, given the latitude of the course and the longitude of the participants.

These guys argue endlessly, criticize style and technique, talk while others of them are teeing off, and accuse one another of breaching golf etiquette. They take merciless advantage. If, enroute to his next shot, one passes by a ball belonging to a companion, he will put his full weight on it, driving it deep into the turf and making it impossible to find. If an undetected little kick will drive a companion's ball into the rough, so it goes. Ollie can send a ball crashing through the woods, emerge from the trees after a brief search, and inexplicably find his ball lying just inside the fairway. "Must have hit a tree and bounced out," is a familiar refrain, and well used. A ball might be picked up by its owner, who's walking toward the green, and be redeposited, clean and polished, twenty feet closer to the pin, the owner having never stopped walking. Homogenized professional golf is boring. These are the guys who ought to be on TV.

One June, they were at the eighth hole, on the homestretch, when Ollie had a little gas. He'd just hit his first shot and, typically, had headed out onto the fairway so he could maneuver his ball around to its best advantage before the others could get close enough to see what he was doing. Suddenly he began clutching and massaging his chest.

"Something's wrong with Ollie," said Bud, the only one who could see that far.

"That's hardly news," responded Woody.

"What if he has a heart attack?" asked Bud.

"I don't think it would affect his game," offered Paul.

"What if it kills him?" queried Woody.

"Leave him lie. The crows will finish him off while we play two more rounds. Next day he'll be back on the course as droppings. It'll save us the trouble of coming up here and scattering his ashes all over the place."

All this banter went on as the other three teed off. Eventually they found themselves out on the fairway with Ollie, who was standing next to his very favorable lie.

"Ollie, you OK? If you're gonna have a spell, don't fall so close to my ball that I can't take a decent shot without hitting your corpse on my follow-through."

"Won't make any difference where I fall 'cause you ain't got any follow-through anyway."

"Don't talk to me about follow-through. That's why none of us came running when you were staggering around out here. We figured, the way you wield an iron and the way the divits were flyin', if you could just hold body and soul together long enough to take this fairway shot you'd already have a good start on your own grave. I don't know why you carry anything in that bag but a shovel."

"Anyway, I think the rules say if something's in your way you can move the ball the length of the club in any direction without suffering a stroke."

"Interesting choice of words, but that's not in the rule book. It's just something that's evolved."

"Well that's more than I can say for the rest of you," said Ollie, continuing, "The rules actually say you can move a loose impediment if the aforesaid impediment is within a club-length of the ball."

"Yeah but is a body a loose impediment?"

"Well yours certainly is," quipped Ollie as he picked up his ball to brush some dirt off it and headed for the green.

⚓ ⚓ ⚓

Down and Out and Counting

Sometimes I drift. My mind wanders, travels compulsively, frequently, spontaneously and of its own accord to a familiar and nearby place where it busies itself counting and averaging, arranging and cataloging. The condition has been diagnosed as Attention Deficit Disorder, but it's hardly disorderly. My mind tidies up and organizes the clutter perceived around it. I sense it's closer to autism or obsessional neurosis, that I missed being one of these special people by just a little. To those close to me it's always apparent when this has happened. It's as though little Out of Order signs, hanging askew, have suddenly appeared where my eyes— moments earlier alert, attentive, and inquiring but now glazed over—had been.

At meetings, where I find myself too often, I'm sometimes useless. Now and then I can be seen from the podium, sitting there with my eyes open but apparently asleep. I'm sure it's disconcerting to the speaker, but while I am not asleep, I *am* engaged elsewhere. I have lost interest in what's going on and am now memorizing the names of the participants and arranging them alphabetically by last name, or first name, maybe by both. If time permits and something doesn't happen to jolt me back to the business at hand I will continue in orbit and assign the alpha characters of their names a numerical value ($A = 1$, $Z = 26$) and then average them. Occasionally I can come up with an acronym from the average for those assembled. At a recent meeting of the, well, never mind, the acronym that emerged was, interestingly, "dithering."

While driving, if conversation is lagging or there's nothing interesting on the radio, I'm soon assigning numerical values to the alpha characters of passing license plates, trying to average them along with the numerical characters and then solving for the resulting two-digit alpha-numeric answer, $293KPL = 5M$ (rounded to the nearest whole number), before the vehicle has passed from view. If you see me coming it would be safer for you and easier for me if you slowed down a little. I usually present a thumbs-up when I've got the answer.

The average height of the seventy-three people encountered during a stroll from one end of Main Street to the other, at around noon on a Tuesday in early August was, I'm guessing about the height, of course, but am sure of the average, five foot eight. These were the adults. I excluded the children, actually tried to do them simultaneously and separately but failed miserably. I made a note to try again next August, but it will have to be at the same time, noon, on the same day, the seventh.

Generally folks don't know that I have this compulsion, an obsessive nature. In fact, the average age of those who do know is fifty-four. This is a fluid number of course, changing now and then as someone else is taken into my confidence. That will change dramatically today, with the publication of these 1,114 words, 212 less than my average this year and 267 less than the average of all my essays.

This year my wife and I lived alone with one another for the first time in eighteen years. Our daughters were away, one at work in Connecticut and the other attending high school in Massachusetts. They kind of excel academically. I like to acknowledge this characteristic by observing to those who commend us on their achievements that each has my mind but is cute like their mother. I think this is funny, funnier than others do, a lot funnier than either girl or her mother does; still, I am not dissuaded. With our daughters gone there was a manageable amount of stuff in the house to obsess over. In the bathroom, for example—the shower specifically—can generally be found the following three categories of things: bars of soap, containers, and implements. During the period from September 6 to June 8, during that time we were alone, a few of each of these things could commonly be found: a couple bars of soap, a couple containers of shampoo or conditioner, and three implements—one of those spongy things on a string, a razor, and a pumice stone. It was a simple matter, hardly challenging, to, while showering, make an orderly presentation of these items, to arrange them alphabetically on one of the several built-in shelves.

Then both daughters came home for the summer. Katie was soon visited by a girlfriend from France and Sarah by two girlfriends from Connecticut. During a shower I began my customary inventory of the vast array of things that had suddenly accumulated and set about the necessary business of creating order from chaos.

"Advanced Strengthening Hydration Therapy Intensive Treatment (makes hair 5 times stronger)." I anguish over a label like that. It's very unsettling, too many words, doesn't lend itself to orderly arranging. But it jolts me back to my senses. Little things do that, they're lifelines to reality. In this case it's the note on the label that says this stuff will make hair five times stronger. Which of these girls wants her hair stronger by a factor of five, and why? Will she become Rapunzel? Will there be island boys heaving themselves up over the windowsills tonight after having ascended hand over hand up the luxurious folds of intensively treated hair? Here is a bottle of "Exfoliating Body Wash." Exfoliating? Is that anything like Agent Orange? Couldn't you accomplish the same thing, and less expensively, with a sea urchin? Does the manufacturer presume to know better than he (she/that) that created us when this protective layer of skin should be removed? "Silk Protein Enriched Shampoo and

Conditioner" and "Clean Rinsing Conditioner for Normal to Oily Hair with Sage, Jasmine and Soy Protein in Mountain Spring Water." I associate protein with meat and fish, sage with seasoning, soy with stir-fry, and mountain spring water with the Coors brewery I visited so often while stationed in Denver. When did these things find their way into shampoo and why? "Shimmering Shower Gel with Glitter" and "Fruit Essentials Body Wash in Juicy Melon or Fresh Peach"—these are frightening terms for a father; they're flavors after all. Jarring encounters like these, with the real world, are the things that tether me here. As soon as the girls come home I intend to line them up alphabetically or perhaps by height, in descending order or maybe ascending, and lay down the law. I will not send my girls off into the world in a shimmering condition, neither glittering, and certainly not wafting of fresh peach or juicy melon.

⚓⚓⚓

My First Time

People tend to wait for the mail with more patience than you would think them capable of. A good crowd, mostly retired folk, gathers at the post office most mornings.

They peer through the little glass windows on their respective mailboxes at the employees on the other side of the wall sorting through stuff and can judge from the activity how near done the process of distributing incoming mail is. This is a familiar group, intimately acquainted with one another and only a little less so with those of us who pop in and out to get our mail or conclude our business. One day my arrival to pick up our mail coincided with that of a woman about my own age. I held the door open for her and, as I did, a memory coughed and sputtered. She bent down to open her post office box.

"You know," I announced to the regulars and pointing to her as she straightened up, "This is the first girl I ever kissed."

She blushed and rushed to assure everyone within earshot that she *remembered nothing of the kind* but did recall that, once, when a bunch of us kids were skating I grabbed her by the arm and tried to guide her into the shadows.

"Why'd I do that?"

"For crying out loud, are you that old? Think about it. All I know is that I'd just gotten a polio shot and my arm was killing me."

I didn't remember that incident but I do remember the kiss.

We sat behind the gym on the steeply sloping ledge with our backs against the building. I was around ten years old, she a little younger. She had on shorts. Legs like a heron's stuck out of them. We each embraced our own drawn-up knees. Our arms afforded some modesty as, with our faces buried in them, we talked about marriage and then about kissing, which, we knew from having watched our parents, had a lot to do with it.

We would kiss, we agreed, but only after we had established a level of commitment, so we agreed to marry when we grew up, that we'd live in the abandoned house that stood right next to where we sat, and that we'd have three children. That settled, we let go of our knees and put our arms on each other's shoulders, and, with our eyes wide open, we kissed. Her fingers were cold where one or two of them touched my neck. So were her lips. My lips were not cold. Nearly cross-eyed, I returned her stare and imagined her thinking, "My, his lips are warm," and I imagined her imagining, "I'll bet he's thinking, 'My, her lips are cold,'" and she'd have been right.

That was a solemn occasion. Our commitment to one another was sober and validated. We rose and walked up the drive to the main street, holding hands and full of the greatness of the moment. Then we turned left and walked a few hundred feet to where she would exit up through Sarah Bunker's yard to her house on the hill. Before we parted, we engaged in an awkward embrace, and I made an effort to bestow another kiss, but just then my Uncle Vic drove by honking his horn to applaud my style. She turned her head and I kissed her hair and part of an ear as it all passed through my lips. My heart was all she could carry as she turned home.

I continued down the hill, across the bridge to my house. People watched and knew they were encountering a different person from the young boy who'd gone up the hill earlier. I had no feet, for example. I glided noiselessly by. And, of course, I had no heart, for, as everyone knows, a young boy moving with no feet has had his heart stolen. I told my parents I had found my mate and about where we planned to live, and, finally, watching them closely, I told about the kiss. They listened carefully and seriously and I knew I was on solid ground.

I'll never forget that afternoon, although it might not have been her after all. It might have been her sister.

⚓ ⚓ ⚓

Away Happens

There are only two places, Here, this island off the coast of Maine, and Away. Here, this place, is a small place and Away, everywhere else, is a big place, but, make no mistake about it, Here is Here and Away is not. One thousand two hundred and seventy-six people live Here. Billions more live Away than live Here, although increasingly, during the summer, it seems otherwise.

There is a big and obvious difference between those who live Here and those who live Away. There is no less a distinction between those who live Here and who the rest of us acknowledge are really from Here and those who live Here but who the rest of us know full well are really from Away.

Each of us is firmly cast one way or the other. We are either from Here or, to one degree or another, we are from Away. These distinctions, some subtle some less so, are laboriously learned and clear to most of us, certainly to those who have been here a couple of generations or more. The understanding among newcomers is, for a while, muddied.

Some cases are clearer than others. A lady who moves Here from Boston in June is still from Away in September. Simple enough. The following year, however, she thinks she's from Here. We all know she's from Away. A few years later she and we are again in agreement. She *is* from Away. At some point she may settle down and send some kids through school, and before you know it she starts thinking she's from Here again, until she succumbs to the temptation to speak up at a school board meeting and discovers she's still from Away.

Other circumstances are far less clear. A couple—for the sake of illumination let's make one of them from Here and the other from Away—settle down Here and have a child, Dolores. Dolores grows up Here, marries a local (different than *from* Here) guy, and they raise a family of their own. Eventually Dolores passes on, having never left. She wasn't *from* Here. She only *was* Here. She was just Here by way of Away. One can only be *from* Here if one and one's ancestors have never lived anywhere else. (If someone named in the Bible is one of those ancestors, it helps.) One cannot *become* from Here.

A person can, however, *become* from Away, and such a stigma is for keeps. There is no redemption, no getting back on the wagon. Away happens. Like many unhappy circumstances, though, being from Away can be improved upon. A person from Away could, for example, marry one of us; and some have, with no more noble purpose than to improve their situation, or to improve the quality of life of those of us who are from here. Either maneuver can be dicey.

I am from Away. This is painful for me to acknowledge but, in the long run, probably therapeutic. My great-great-great-great-great-grandfather, James Roberts, landed here on Vinalhaven Island among other early settlers in 1792. He married Sarah Hall from Matinicus Island, a variation of Away but not as bad as, say, Worcester. They raised fifteen kids. One of them was my great-great-great-great-grandfather William Roberts. He and his wife had James II, who married Jane Shaw, whose picture hangs in my dining room. They had Hannibal Hamlin Roberts, who married Aura Marcella Coombs and fathered Rena, my great-grandmother, the matriarch of five living generations until she died in 1989 at age one hundred and one. Rena was the mother of my grandmother Phyllis, and there the trouble began.

In 1923, when Gram was sixteen, a crewman on the old *Governor Bodwell,* a passenger steamer serving mainland Rockland and the offshore islands of Vinalhaven, North Haven, Isle A Haut, Stonington, and Swans Island, a man from Away, stopped Here and swept her off her feet. She remained aloft with Ted Maddox during their sixty-five years together and then, after his death, for another fifteen years until she passed away herself in 2000. When newly married, however, after my mother had been born Here, they removed themselves to Boston, an impulsive and ill-considered move. Bad enough she'd taken up with a man from Away, but to go there with him. . . . My mother went to school in Boston and married my father, her high-school sweetheart. They had me and then my brother Dick, and in 1948, after my Dad's service in Germany in World War II, both they and my Grampa Ted and Gram Phyllis, each by now either originally from Away or having become so, came back to the island where the two men went into business together. Eventually I became the eldest of four brothers, the last two of whom were born Here. They are from Away too, of course, but less so than me. When I'm traveling and folks ask me where I'm from I tell them Vinalhaven, Maine. Out Here they know better.

In June the Lions Club nominating committee made it's annual presentation to the membership, reporting out a recommended slate of officers for the ensuing year.

"The Committee proposes the following candidates," invoked the chair. "For president, Paul Rhoads. For vice presi——"

"Rhoads!" exclaimed one longtime member in disgust, "I remember when they first come here, during the Depression. He's from Away and so's his woman. I don't mean no offense, Paul, I think you're finest kind of fella', 'specially being from Away and all, but a transplant as King Lion? I don't hardly think so."

"Jeez, Rolly, most of us here are from Away at one time or another," replied the startled committee chair, a fellow only a couple of generations removed from Away. "Even you, now that I think about it. Your father came back Here with you after your real mother run off and left him up to Worcester, but you was almost school age by then."

"Yea," volunteered Randy, piling on, "and we all remember when your stepmother run away and lived with that rope salesman over in Warren. She stayed there for fifteen years, long enough for any Vinalhaven she had in her to wear pretty damn thin."

Rolly had opened the floodgates and now he had to defend himself. "My people have roots Here all the way back to when this place was first settled. That's more than damn near any of you can say."

"Roots ain't good enough, Rolly, and you know it. There might have been an Austin here in the beginning but there wasn't a sign of 'em for a good long spell till your old man brought you back here."

"Well," says Max, "I agree with Rolly. I say we hadn't ought to have folks in leadership positions like King Lion or town manager and so on unless they're really from Here. How about a point system. If you were born Here you get ten points. Then——"

"Wait a minute. Nobody's born Here anymore. They're all born over to the hospital nowadays."

"Well, you know what I mean."

"I don't know what you mean, never have for that matter."

"I mean you woulda' been born Here if they was still deliverin'. Anyway, if your mother or father was born Here you get another ten points each. If their folks was all born Here you get ten points each, and so forth all the way back. Anyone whose ancestors settled Here back in the 1700s and whose descendants never left can credit 9 or 10 generations.

That's a maximum of five thousand points or so. And then, for every instance of dilution, let's call it, ten points is subtracted. So if your great grandfather got himself a woman from up in Springfield, subtract ten points. If your grandmother went off to work in Boston and never came back till she retired, lose another ten points. If your folks are from Here and you were born Here but you look an awful lot like a particular summer fella, another ten points lost. Seems like an accumulation of four thousand points ought to clinch it."

The membership settled down to compute relative nativeness and discovered that none of them came remotely close. Upon further examination, they could identify only one person in town who was really *from* Here, and he had an odd and distracting twitch.

I'm from Away and I am beginning to deal with it. Sometimes I stand up in a crowded restaurant and announce, "Hi. My name is Phil and I'm from Away." More and more often folks applaud and offer encouragement.

⚓ ⚓ ⚓

Passing the Peace

Newly arrived in Vinalhaven our new minister was seized at the pulpit by the notion that everyone in the congregation could be made to feel as warm and fuzzy as he did at that moment. He stepped out from behind the pulpit, clasped his hands together, looked at us in earnest, and said: "People, I want you to take the hand of the person sitting next to you. I want you to look them in the eye. I want you to speak their name and I want you to say to them, 'Your life has been a blessing to me.'"

We were all so stunned by the prospect that there resulted a moment during which nothing happened except the soundless individual calculations of how easily one might make an exit while attention was diverted. Undeterred, the minister spun around, grabbed the organist's hand in both of his, and, with a depth of feeling we all felt ashamed not to emulate, spoke her name and said, "Your life has been a blessing to me," to which was gulped the appropriate response. The motion required to pass this message among us then began. First we all had to rise to our feet, which produced a comfortably distracting but short-lived noise. For some time now the congregation had engaged in an exchange of greetings and we'd adopted a procedure for this awkward phase of the service that had, until this morning, only required us to exchange pleasantries. We usually stand and then turn around to extend our hand and administer our blessings to the person seated behind us. This produces another momentary respite, because that person (if there's anyone there) has turned backward to do the same thing. The result is that for a while everyone in the congregation is facing the occupants of the back row. On this day, accordingly, the folks in the next-to-the-last row back extended their hands to the back benchers and said, "Your life has been a blessing to me." Then they turned around to face the rest of us and extended their greetings to those seated in front of them, and the ripple thus given birth wafted across the congregation like "the wave" through the bleachers at Fenway Park. My time is quickly coming. I'm only a few pews from the back. In a moment I'll be turning around to extend my hand to the people in front of me and, oh, why couldn't I have come in late. I can't even remember who is sitting in front of me. I never noticed. The older woman who is seated behind me turns around and extends her tiny hand to me. She is seated with her daughter. Thankfully they are both fond of me, I having befriended them once or twice. They say "Phil, your life has been a blessing to me," and I feel OK; they mean it. I say the same thing to them, and in so doing I learn that if you both speak simultaneously there's really no sure way of telling if the other person has said exactly what was required. I might have said, "Your life has been a blessing to me," and they might have been saying, "You have a great big piece of spinach hanging from your teeth and your fly is open." I turn to face the people in the pew in front of me, no doubt waiting expectantly. As I turn I encounter my wife's gaze, she turning with me, and I think, why not just tell her that her life has been a blessing to me and let it go at that. I *could* say it to someone for whom I mean it. But no, we continue to turn until we are face to face with a very somber looking lady, my mother's age.

One fall day when I was around thirteen this same lady emerged from her snug house to collect an armful of fuel from the woodshed. Inside, on a bench covered with blankets, a makeshift examining table, lay her twelve-year-old daughter, the patient, undergoing a critical examination by myself. I had on a smock fashioned from a sheet and was making liberal use of the stethoscope, which had come with the doctor's kit I'd gotten the Christmas before.

The woman hasn't spoken to me in the ensuing forty years. I take her hand in mine and say, "Your life has been a blessing to me."

She mumbles something in response. It's probably better I don't know.

The ordeal concluded, I search among the unoccupied pews for a place to occupy next Sunday, a new spot, a seat that will spare her and myself suffering this anguish again. I find a place, a seat around which are sitting a few benign folks, people with whom I always exchange pleasantries and small talk.

A week later I enter the church and sit down in my new place. Here and there, scattered throughout this new "neighborhood," are folks with whom I have no quarrel. Just before services begin I sense people seating themselves right behind me. I wait. I worry. At the appointed time I stand and face the back of the church, as does the couple behind me—my first wife's parents.

In the Name of the Father and of Saving Time

If you position an Aim'n'Flame so its tip is adjacent to the tip of your index finger, and the barrel is aligned along the inside of that finger, and the trigger is just beneath the ball of your thumb, and the rest of the handle is tucked up under your cuff, you can point that index finger at something, like a candle, and, by depressing the trigger with your inverted middle finger (it takes practice), you can produce a flame that appears, to those of your audience who are on the other side of the aforementioned finger, to emerge from your fingertip, and you can light that candle. The effect is pretty magical, but if you are a minister and are lighting the candles on the altar the effect is profound. It is these depths to which Pastor Bob descends without hesitation, and it is these gimmicks with which he holds his congregation spellbound. It's also a time-saving exercise: no need to find a little kid to light each candle and recite something appropriate; no need to try and get damp matches to light. In the interest of saving time, precious minutes during which he can extend his sermon, Bob is thinking of other ways to save largely ceremonial time during the service. The latest involves communion and it may be over the edge. He has a super soaker and he has wine.

⚓ ⚓ ⚓

Raising the Bar

I was surprised but delighted to be invited to a wine tasting. I don't think I'm known as a cultural wasteland, but neither am I very well acquainted with much of what passes for sophistication, namely literature, music, art, and wine. That is not to say I don't make an effort now and then.

As regards literature, I keep going to poetry readings even though I don't seem to be acquiring a taste for it, not contemporary compositions anyway. On those occasions the reader, often the poet, moves me, but rarely the poem. I'm a little ashamed—I don't know exactly why, but I sense I should be—to admit that I like poems that rhyme and that I can understand, not the poems found, for example, in the *New Yorker*. They don't rhyme. Neither do I understand them. Further, they seem to rely on distractions, on the misuse of punctuation and grammar, to lend a heft the poem might not otherwise impart. I like "The Psalm of Life" by Longfellow.

Music, classical music actually, a proper appreciation of which would go a long way toward giving me a loftier perch from which to regard the world, just doesn't resonate with me, although I keep going to the concerts. There's a staggering amount of music out here on the islands. I love most of it: blues, gospel, doo-wop, bluegrass—but classical music, well—again it's the performer I enjoy, particularly a pianist or a string player, someone whose face, free of the instrument, can be watched. I used to carry a clarinet in the school band here on the island. I say "carry" because that is the only acknowledgment the music teacher would give to my participation. I was not a good clarinetist. When we marched on Memorial Day he, having removed the reed from my clarinet, told me to puff out my cheeks when I marched by my unsuspecting family so they could beam proudly like the parents of the kids who were really playing their instruments.

I'm trying harder with art because my wife Elaine is a successful and enthusiastic painter. Sometimes I go to museums or galleries and look at paintings. The truth? I like Norman Rockwell. Not much of the other stuff moves me. The Mona Lisa? I've seen more beguiling smirks—this week. There are exceptions though. That one Michelangelo did of God, for example, was pretty good, and, of course, I love all my wife's paintings.

I've done better with wine. It was because of my association with Elaine that I got to go to the wine tasting. She was invited and I kind of "go with her," like Kleenex. It wasn't long ago that I couldn't tolerate wine, couldn't fathom what folks saw in the stuff. Beer was great, coffee too. Either, I felt, enhanced a meal and I'd enjoyed both for decades. But wine! It just tasted awful and it was expensive. You could get three or four six packs of Schaefer for what it cost for one jug of wine. Not long ago, though, a short-lived and modest affluence descended on me, and as I prospered I felt I needed wine. The awareness came on very naturally—like the feeling I had at around thirteen that I needed a girl-friend, and later, at around seventeen, that I needed one quite desperately. I was evolving. Suddenly, I liked wine, all kinds of wine, and I began to buy it by the box. I began to do more entertaining and to feel more confident about having folks over, different folks, more cosmopolitan folks. Right away I'd offer them a glass of wine, and go right to the refrigerator and fill a glass from the little tap on the box, and I'd refresh their glasses similarly as required. Sometimes our guests would comment about the wine, something like "Mmm, interesting," and I could tell that theirs was not an unqualified endorsement, so I'd answer with something like "Perhaps it hasn't had a chance to breathe, it's such a short walk from the fridge." Soon, though, we began to receive bottles of wine as gifts and our guests would bring bottles to dinner themselves. Gradually, as I consumed more and more of it, I was able to actually distinguish those I enjoyed from those I enjoyed less, or more, and I had to acknowledge that I liked them *all* better than the stuff in the box in the fridge. I needed to learn more, and I like to be orderly when I learn about things, so I first learned there were reds and whites. The simplicity of this first step pleased me, and I'm glad I took the time because my particular color blindness would otherwise surely have resulted, at some point, in my going to Island Spirits and asking for a nice, mauve Merlot to present to my hostess.

Now, having had a little experience, although I don't know a Reisling from a Chardonnay or a Pinot Noir from a Cabernet Sauvignon, I am less nervous when eating out. I look at the wine list as soon as I'm seated so I'll be ready. I pick out a white wine that is about four dollars a glass and whose name I can pronounce, and when the waitperson asks if I'd like a drink to start I order that glass of wine. There is one exception. If Gewurztraminer is among the selections, and if it's available by the glass, I order it regardless because I love to say "Gewurztraminer." I took German in high school for the same reason: I loved the sound of the language. I wasn't good at that either. I sort of carried the language, like the clarinet, instead of speaking it. Several years later, while in the service, I met a German girl on the beach in Marseille and, intending to invite her (in her own language) to dinner, I instead challenged her to "stand up against the bathroom wall and hold a sheet of paper between her teeth while waving her arms in the universal sign of alarm." She seemed to pick up on the alarm part, but not much else about my proposal interested her.

When I choose a full bottle from the menu I select a red wine with a red meat dish and a white with everything else, and, again, if I can pronounce it and it costs around twenty dollars I order it. A twenty-dollar bottle seems to impress everyone just enough.

The alert that a wine tasting was in the offing came printed on a piece of heavy chartreuse paper with those irregular and seemingly worn edges that are so popular nowadays, the kind that look like so many of the paper goods left to winter over in summer homes and which the squirrels have been enjoying. I say "alert" because the invitation was addressed to Elaine.

Added, apparently as an afterthought and in a different ink, was "and Phil," the subtle implication being that she might put the intervening week to good use by bringing me up to speed regarding appropriate wine-tasting etiquette. Inside were the details and a handwritten note offering the opportunity to make a contribution. "We're asking each guest to bring a wrapped palette refresher to be enjoyed between tastings," it read, "Surprise us!" Boy, I thought, this is pretty exciting, and I headed for the pantry to be sure we had plenty of smoked kippers in Louisiana Hot Sauce.

⚓ ⚓ ⚓

The Wedding Planner

There is much to be said for versatility and Jeff has it in spades. He came to the island fifteen years ago claiming he could do anything, and the truth has borne him out. He can't do anything for long but he can, in fact, do anything. Right now it's summer and Jeff has become, with the same indefatigable focus and energy he's brought to every short-lived undertaking, a marketing consultant. The impetus for this fleeting interest took root as Jeff was leafing through an issue of *Modern Bride*, a shameless and weighty publication that caters to the astonishing needs of prospective brides in and around New York City with so much glitz that it makes *Vogue* look like *Popular Mechanics*. Someone had left it at the motel, and I, in turn, deposited it at the Hardware Store for the enlightenment of the little group of men who gather there each day.

Jeff recognized that Vinalhaven has, in recent years, become a popular spot for couples whose idea of the perfect wedding is a little less grandiose than those touted in *Modern Bride*, but he was also quick enough to acknowledge the undeniable appeal of certain goods and services, such as those offered in the magazine under the heading "That Special Touch That Will Make Your Wedding Day Even More Memorable." The opportunity to cash in on this lucrative market by modifying such nuptial amenities to more closely reflect island values revealed itself to him with the same clarity that accompanied his idea last summer having to do with the aforementioned little knot of Hardware Store curmudgeons. His idea was to transform these fellows, who contrast so strikingly with the annoyingly cheerful greeter at WalMart, into personal shoppers for the summer people.

In June, Jeff pitched his idea of transforming Vinalhaven into a Mecca for island weddings at the Chamber of Commerce meeting. His presentation was delayed until after happy hour, dinner (more drinks), and the regular business meeting, all of which helped grease the ways, as it were. By the first of August, his considerable advance in hand, Jeff was pushing for involvement in a Gift Registry so hard and regular at the door of each chamber member that he might as well have been in labor.

One of the most singularly striking services offered in the "Special Touch" section of *Modern Bride* was the Dove Release. Several companies offer this service, whereby, through a sliding hatch in the top of a truck, they release, at a significant moment, a bevy, for tens of thousands of dollars, or (for the bride on a budget) a covey, for a few thousand dollars, of doves, each trailing a ribbon (color to be chosen by the bride).

As it happens, seagulls routinely get themselves momentarily trapped and confused in the fenced-in confines of the motel decks (where else can island newlyweds honeymoon?), and it didn't take Jeff long to make the imaginative transition. He tied up a handful of gulls, each with pot warp, and quickly perfected the desired effect with the release of a sheep shank around each leg. He had a novelty shop make up some little yellow sou'westers and fastened one loosely to each gull's head with one of those little elastics girls use in their hair. Thus attired, they made quite a jaunty little covey, and the practice run held forth the promise of a fine nuptial accompaniment. As for picking the moment—well, this is a motel after all. A moment of significance could certainly be agreed upon; determining it's precise occurrence from a remote location was another matter. Jeff discovered while practicing that the term "bird release" took on a much broader meaning, especially if said gulls were confined and required to keep their hats on for very long.

We anticipate a busy and profitable wedding season.

⚓⚓⚓

This Town Ain't Big Enough for Both of 'em

$\int$ ome ATV riders are riding their machines up and down Main Street at the same time the policeman is supposed to be riding his machine up and down Main Street. This results in overcrowding and cannot continue. Please follow this schedule:

ATV's

Mon.	all day
Tues.	all day
Wed.	all day
Thur.	12:01 A.M.–noon
	10 P.M.–midnight
Fri.	12:01 A.M.–2 P.M.
Sat.	12:01 A.M.–4 P.M.

POLICE

Thur.	noon–10 P.M.
Fri.	2 P.M.–midnight
Sun.	12:01 A.M.–2 A.M.
	2 P.M.–midnight

Riders in either case should try to avoid one another, and while the police have done so dutifully, the same cannot be said for the ATV riders, who are often riding even as the policeman is getting off the ferry to begin a tour of duty. This is risky and, though it has never been known to happen, might lead to arrest.

⚓ ⚓ ⚓

Summer Visitors' Night

Just beneath the surface in most men there lurks a real grub. My wife offered this wry observation after I described to her the behavior of the men in attendance at the most recent annual stag lobster feed, hosted for over fifty years now by the Vinalhaven Lions. Long referred to as Summer Visitors' Night, it is unclear whether this banquet celebrates the fact that its honorees are here among us or, given its customary August date, that they will soon be gone. There are Lions Clubs in nearly every country in the world, and it's characteristic of them all to celebrate some local but otherwise insignificant event with a feast at which is featured an indigenous culinary specialty. In a certain Vermont town, for example, the running of the sap is celebrated at a pancake breakfast with maple syrup. A club just outside Manila annually commemorates the durability of the water buffalo with roasted horns of the animal stuffed with a combination of marrow and fly larvae. In an Iranian village, poached sheep eyes are served to men honoring their own virility. On Vinalhaven lobster is king.

About fifteen years ago a particularly sophisticated member (the club welcomes seasonal residents as well as islanders) with four daughters and no sons proposed that the Summer Visitors' Night be a coed affair. He was taken to the back of the Lions Den and subjected to an archaic embarrassment upon which, as a member, I am not permitted to elaborate. He was then stripped of his membership on the Marching and Chowder Committee and not allowed to sing the club song until his recantation had been recorded in the minutes. That same year the Supreme Court found the Elks guilty of violating the civil rights of women seeking membership in their lodge, and Lions International (headquarters) forthwith adopted a coed policy toward membership. Now only the Vinalhaven club and one or two in Iran are still stag.

I sat at Grimes Park with eighty or so other men at wooden picnic tables on a comfortable evening. The park is a peninsula named for Fred Grimes, the man who bequeathed it to the Cassie Coombs Woodcock American Legion Post. The Post's continued existence is due largely to the women who are among its ranks and who graciously allow the Lions to observe their annual affair unhampered by the debt they owe these women or by the burden of political correctness that has brought so many men's groups to their knees. Among them were islanders and summer visitors alike. Caretakers, U.S. Senators, grocers, men whose usual Christmas bonus is larger than the town's annual budget, ministers, Walter Cronkite, municipal employees, authors, carpenters, innkeepers, movie actors, lobstermen, university professors, garbagemen, publishers, teachers—over the years they've all been guests at Summer Visitors' Night. This year was no exception.

We sit amid piles of lobster, mussels, and young corn,

all steamed to perfection; so much food that it sometimes obstructs our view of one another as we settle naturally into gluttonous excess. A ravenous madness ensues. The pace quickens; a sort of anxiety builds. Lobster tails are ripped from bodies, their contents expelled in a practiced maneuver, nearly staggering in its eroticism were it not for the casual and detached manner in which it is executed. Claws are similarly separated and smashed with rocks or sticks, broken in pieces with bare hands often bloodied in the process, or simply chomped through by the rapacious diners. Great gaping maws already overflowing with the world's best white meat and more melted butter than they would have been allowed at home in a lifetime are crammed further full. We've each been given a napkin, a nod to civility, but a joke. A napkin would have no more impact on the mess we're making than duct tape on a bomb crater. A few newcomers have pathetically tucked their napkins into their necks like bibs. We seasoned gourmands use our sleeves, or our bare arms. A frenzy of consumption is under way that would make hyenas around a fallen wildebeest look like dinner with Martha Stewart.

And then, just as it seems we might be capable of devouring our own young, the danger passes. A level of satiation is reached and joke and story telling begins. Remarkably, the words ooze in understandable form through and around half chewed globs of succulence, some of which are unavoidably expelled along with the words themselves. No matter. Faces smattered with pieces of white gelatinous stuff break into appreciative smiles and beards and mustaches dripping with butter move with mouths forming grins. Laughter has begun; uproarious laughter; medicinal, restorative. Sides ache wonderfully bad; tears of glee run skimming off buttered whiskers like water off a duck's ass. Someone could choke to death trying to feed on this level and talk and laugh at the same time. Again, no matter. It would be worth it. If everyone could laugh like this for a few minutes at the beginning of each day there'd be no wars.

It would be different with women there. We're not being unfaithful. We're just being grubs. I hope the Supreme Court doesn't find out about us.

⚓ ⚓ ⚓

Four-Letter Words

Four-letter words have insinuated themselves into the lives of my family. They've settled comfortably into the fabric of the lives of my wife and our daughters but they're unsettling to me. They use these words—actually there are only two words (so far)—freely. Not only do they use the words without hesitation, but they employ both the technique described by one word and the substance of the other freely as well, and (this is the troubling part) they are unabashedly trying to introduce these terms and their respective concepts into *my* life. The offending words are yoga and tofu. I sometimes stumble, in my house, over a woman who has assembled herself in an unlikely and uncomfortable-looking pose, appearing very much like someone who has fallen down and who, because she has apparently broken several things, cannot get up again and whose helpless form a devilish passerby has twisted further askew with legs emerging from where arms should be and the reverse. Since they position themselves often and for sustained periods in my path, I assume they are subliminally suggesting that I, prompted no doubt by my natural grace and flexibility, become a yoga disciple.

We have recently taken to dining by candlelight, a coy move I thought was intended to put me in a receptive mood. Not so. Instead it was thought that in dim light I could not distinguish between the tasty morsels I enjoy and those gelatinous blobs of tofu trying to pass themselves off as chicken. If God had meant for us to eat tofu why did he give us teeth? It's like trying to chew the stuff that congeals around a canned ham, like trying to land a punch in a dream; there is nothing there. Why, for that matter, did he give us taste buds? Certainly not so we could more fully appreciate tofu. If it's cooked with chicken it tastes like chicken. If it's cooked with fish it tastes like fish. I have a better idea: chicken and fish.

⚓ ⚓ ⚓

Friendly Fire

This summer down at the motel was kind of typical. Early one evening I was summoned by a guest about to depart for dinner, who complained of a loud scratching noise coming from the area beneath the shower. The Tidewater is built right over the water in Carver's Harbor, and mink and raccoons come down from the pond above and live among the grout and granite fill that is Main Street in Vinalhaven. Underneath the motel is a crawl space, a foot or two high, running the entire length of the building. It can be accessed from each room through a little trapdoor that exposes the plumbing beneath each tub and shower unit. It is directly under each of these bathrooms, lined up in a straight row, where the coons and mink have beaten down a path through the insulation to create their main thoroughfare from one end of the motel to the other. I wouldn't mind if they ran back and forth forever. Unfortunately they use it as a rest stop too. For a long time we had maintained a trap under the bathroom in number 4. I knew that the noise complained of was a critter caught in the trap and didn't relish the prospect of dealing with it.

I went down to the motel and got out of the truck with a

loaded pistol in my hand. Usually it's fall or winter when this sort of thing occurs and the motel is either empty or occupied by workmen or some other particular population, men mostly, and likely to be less troubled by the prospect of the motel manager arriving with a loaded gun. This was August. The motel was full and all our guests were out and about the premises, going or coming or lingering and chatting happily with one another. The young man and woman in unit 4, the ones who had called about the scratching noise, had sheepishly confided to my wife earlier in the day that they had left their wallet in their car on the mainland. Elaine was perfectly willing, as we always are, to let them finish the rest of their stay with us, and even lent them some cash to spend while they were here. Word of this hospitable gesture quickly spread among our other guests. My appearance with the gun led them all to think I might not be as accommodating as Elaine. As I let myself into number 4 with the master key in one hand and the gun in the other, I became aware of an eerie quiet around me. The doors to the other units— they could each have been saloons—were either closed, with the occupants peering out from between drawn curtains, or were open just a crack, with eyes piled on top of one another amid whispers of "They came without money" and "This must be the husband." A few minutes after I closed the door behind me, three shots rang out. We have a dozen rooms. About half our guests had prepaid. When I emerged from the room the other half were all lined up at the lobby offering to do the same.

One winter when Elaine and I were out of town my father was looking after the place for us. A coon again got caught in the trap under number 4. Dad went in to dispatch it the same way. After removing the trapdoor he could not see the animal, which had hidden itself behind some plumbing. He couldn't risk shooting around all that plumbing, so he stuck in his head and torso, holding the gun in one hand and a flashlight in the other. It was a tiny access door, allowing him barely room to move. I wouldn't have done it, but Dad's an old World War II veteran and afraid of nothing. He located the coon, put it out of its misery, damn near deafening himself in the process, and began working to extricate himself. While so doing, he heard a hissing sound on his left and laboriously turning in that direction, he found himself face to face with another coon, this one bearing down on him at full speed. He couldn't get himself into position to use the gun or even to defend himself. The animal jumped up onto his head, ran down his back, squeezed between his butt and the edge of the access hole, and went on into the motel room where it found itself alone with my dad's hindquarters. The image, and its potential for serious consequences, was not lost on him. He made a hasty exit, tearing his clothes and himself on offending nails and screws on the way out, and was much relieved to find that the critter had climbed the headboard. Several rounds were required to dispatch it, one of which traveled through the wall and, having by then lost all of its momentum, lodged in the drapes of the room next door. No one was hurt; the occupants of the adjoining room had long since retreated in the face of so much gun fire.

We pay our cleaning ladies quite a bit more than nearly any other Maine motel. They earn it.

In August, a couple of schoolteachers booked a room with us, first timers. Emma and Gail made a big deal over how personable they found the island, how friendly everyone was, how everyone spoke to them, how intimate the town seemed, how friendly, really. They needed to catch the early boat the morning of their departure, and Gail asked for a wake-up call. There are no phones in the room. Early the next morning I peeked (I guess that's a bad choice of a word) in through the curtain they'd carelessly left ajar and saw that they were still asleep, Gail in the double bed nearest the water and Emma in the single nearest me. I opened the door with my master key and tiptoed over to Gail's bed. I bent over her, took her by the shoulders, and gave a gentle shake.

"Wake up Gail, time to get up," I whispered. She stirred and began a stretch that threatened to be a little sensuous. I interrupted it with a little kiss on the cheek and said, a little more firmly, "5:30, Gail, time to get up." Behind me Emma gasped. Frankly she startled me a little. She'd evidently awoken a moment earlier and seemed to be having a hard time believing her eyes. "Uh, Gail," she said in a loud voice, never taking her eyes off me and seeming not to care a whit about how gradually and gently Gail came fully awake. Gail's eyes flew open. "Good morning Phil," she mumbled, clutching her bedclothes up around her neck. "Well, there," I said, "That's better. Now you ladies get yourselves dressed and what not and I'll go out and get you some coffee."

Later, as I gave them a ride down to the ferry, they confided that they'd never experienced quite this level of personal service at any other motel. Well, that's the difference between people out here and those elsewhere. We're friendly, really.

⚓ ⚓ ⚓

Doing Hair

In the course of running the motel, I've wandered in and out of adjacent Hair Heaven over the years and, unlike similar exposures elsewhere and at other times, the lessons learned have not been entirely lost on me. On the contrary, I have assimilated a great deal, not only as an observer of the cutting and styling techniques employed but also as an unintentional eavesdropper on the other side of the skimpy wall that has separated Hair Heaven and its exceedingly talkative patrons from the motel lobby. Accordingly, because Hair Heaven is leaving, and because I can't bear the thought of a summer without the unmistakable aroma of a perm-in-progress wafting through the lobby, I've decided to become a part-time hairdresser. Further, I expect to retain Hair Heaven's former clientele, and I suggest to those among you who may feel otherwise that you think carefully before making a hasty decision to abandon ship. You might, for example, consider the consequences of an accidental spillage, as it were, of the surreptitiously shared secrets, knowledge of which I innocently acquired, during the aforementioned unintentional eavesdropping. Enough said. Suffice my assurance that your intimacies will continue to be safe with us here at Hair Hell as long as you remain our faithful patrons.

Special this week: *Men's Back to Summer Whizbangs.* $6.99. Please line up outside next to the hose. The attendant (probably Dave Wooster) will tend to your shampoo. You can speed things along if, after your wash, you towel-dry and arrange one of the nearby Cool Whip containers on your head in such a way as to expose only what you'd like removed.

⚓⚓⚓

Culture Shock

Sometimes it takes a little while for us out here on the islands to catch up with what's fashionable elsewhere in the world. Take the spoken word for example. A tribe of heretofore undiscovered folks was found living in Borneo not long ago. Eventually translated, their remarks relative to their discoverers were found to be: "He's, like, hairy," "She's, like, cute," and "They're, like, appetizing; I wonder if they're, like, range-fed." Even these primitive people were quicker to use *like* in this particular adverbial way than we were. Similarly, it took island youngsters quite a while longer to use the simultaneously inflected and deflected "Duh" as an automatic response to queries from adults that the rest of the world's juveniles have employed to such effect for so long. Nowadays we do *like* and *Duh* pretty routinely, but it somehow lacks the legitimacy it enjoys elsewhere. Still other of the world's habits just never do catch on. You never hear anyone say to an island woman heading "out to haul," "You go girl." As this lobster-fishing community has become increasingly a tourist destination we struggle more and more with the rest of the world's social graces.

For instance, a new restaurant that opened up had itself a maitre d' and its own bartender and everything. They had a lot of live music, and as a result the place was quite a draw some nights. Still, they tapped the locals as waitresses and waiters, and these folks, capable enough in familiar surroundings, were sometimes hard-pressed to conduct themselves in ways that fit the notion of "service" to which some of our visitors were accustomed. Now you take the matter of wine selection and related details. The owners had put together a reasonable wine list with the help of the distributor's customer service people, but they lacked follow-through. One day, when the place was absolutely packed, one of our homegrown young ("You go girl") women, particularly harried, just done with a long day stuffing bait bags, found herself waitressing the dinner shift on open-mike night. At table eleven was seated a cosmopolitan young couple who'd come over from the motel and had already determined that the only way to ensure solicitous service was to make a fairly big and demanding noise and sustain it at a good shrill pace. Circumstances on this night were clearly going to require an elevated level of such demands, as the place was so crowded and was staffed by so many indigenous people of such limited capabilities. Shirley asked them if they had made a drink selection and they responded with an interrogation sufficient to establish her everlasting inadequacy in such matters. The stage set, they asked to speak to the wine steward in person. Shirley reported back to the bartender.

Scooter had *The Bartender's Guide* attached to the wall with duct tape above the opening in the little bar through which he could view the completely packed dining room. In way over his head and not in an agreeable frame of mind, he stormed across the dining room, gathering his wits about him only as he neared his destination.

"Can I help you folks?" he inquired.

"Only if you've experienced, like, civilization at some point in your, like, life"—the young diner snickered as if to emphasize the wild abandon he employed in painting "life" with such a broad stroke.

"Let me try," replied Scooter, a bemedaled Vietnam vet who was working three jobs to support a family of his own that included three orphaned kids he and Ruthie had adopted at midlife. "Our house wine this evening is a lovely Chilean Chablis, deep but not too demanding," he began, "kind of the opposite of you."

Over the cries of, "Hey, Scooter, how about another pitcher of Bud and some more wings?" the sparring continued, eventually subsiding as the ruffled young man selected a Sauvignon to go with their lobster. By this time the room had quieted down as more and more diners, a lot of them islanders, tuned in to the entertaining exchange. Scooter returned to his station.

For years Scooter had admired the technique employed by wine stewards in nice restaurants as they casually made a classy little corkscrew appear from nowhere, effortlessly opened a bottle of wine tableside, and poured a little for the lead diner to sample. But Scooter only had one of those big corkscrews they sell at the IGA with the two handles that come up like wings. The restaurant had only been open a few days and he'd been carrying the gizmo around in his jeans pocket in anticipation of the opportunity to employ it at his own first tableside ceremony. Scooter liked to think he still cut a pretty classy figure, and the first thing he poured in his new bartending job was himself into his old 505 Straight Cut Levis instead of the 550 Comfort Fit jeans Ruthie had recently begun buying for him. He was a devoted husband and father but a consummate flirt, he couldn't help himself. He imagined the dining room full of admiring women. How was he to know that they were looking at the impression of the corkscrew in his pocket?

The first occasion he'd had to open a bottle tableside was for six elementary teachers, all married but notorious for going out once a month or so without their husbands, blowing off a little steam, and engaging in a few crude indulgences. In Scooter, as he struggled to pull the enormous corkscrew from his pants, they found their mark. He retrieved it, but not before he'd occasioned a wince or two, as a few pushes were required to disentangle the point from the fabric deep in his pocket. Maneuvering himself into a position where he could open the bottle, he scooched down a little, stuck the bottle between his legs, inserted the corkscrew, wound it in, and then employed both hands to bring down the handles. When he pulled out the cork the bottle sought the most natural escape from the grip of his thighs, slipped between his legs and fell to the floor. As it happens it landed upright, and so grateful were the ladies for the ribald amusement they'd derived from the occasion that it wouldn't have mattered if he'd spilled it all over them.

Scooter had since taken to practicing at home and wasn't about to attempt any more tableside service until he'd perfected his technique so, in this case, he opened the New York Cabernet Sauvignon for number eleven back at the bar and gave it to Shirley to take to the table. When she arrived with it, the young gentleman gave her a withering look of disdain and said, "This wine is supposed to be opened at the table. Having been opened at the bar, it has breathed excessively and has now lost much of the subtle nuance we might have expected from it."

"No shit," said Shirley as she put the bottle to her lips, inverted it completely, and took a big healthy swig. Wiping a little dribble from the corner of her mouth and modestly dispensing with a tiny pocket of gas, she pronounced, "Hell, this is finest kind, hasn't lost any of its nuisance at all. Now you folks drink up and enjoy your lobster, 'cause the boat don't leave till mornin'."

⚓ ⚓ ⚓

Exploring the Westkeag Estuary with a White Owl

My neighbor Roy hadn't spent much time on the water. Born, raised, and still living on Vinalhaven as was I, he was nonetheless strictly a landlubber and made no bones about it. I, on the other hand, while actually having spent very little time on the water, was convinced I had Yamalube in my veins. When a friend for whom I was building a house left his twenty-five foot Mako Whaler in my "care," I wasn't long in finding an excuse to use it. I headed across the street to Roy's and, feigning exquisite nonchalance, offered him a boat ride.

"Where we goin?" he asked.

Where indeed. What the hell difference does it make where we're goin'? Did he want to go for a boat ride or not, I sputtered to myself.

"Thomaston," I replied impatiently, indicating a coastal community fifteen miles distant.

"What for?" he queried, as if it were any of his business.

"I have to pick up something at Jeff's Marine."

"Why not have it sent over on the ferry?"

"Geez! 'Cause I want to go for a boat ride; you wanna come or not?"

"How long's it going to take?" he asked stuffing four or five packs of White Owl cigars into his pocket.

"I figure about an hour, tops."

"You know how to get there?" He raised an eyebrow as he filled a cooler from behind the counter in his workshop.

"Course I know how to get there," I snorted contemptuously. "What can there be but to go to Rockland and take a left. After that the first right's got to be the St. George River, upstream from which is Thomaston."

We cast off around 9 A.M. I noticed the tide was pretty near low. Roy stuck a White Owl in his teeth, filled a cup from his cooler, and stood next to me at the center console. I pushed her in the corner and Roy reached for the windshield to support himself. By the time the twin 150 H.P. Mercs had us planed out, the fire that moments before had been just warming up the end of his cigar was working on Roy's lips. Unable to get his teeth unclenched or loose his grip on the windshield, he flung the drink into his face, extinguishing the fire. The sodden stub and ash clung to the stubble on his chin.

In minutes we'd covered the eight miles to Owl's Head Peninsula and I accordingly hung a left into Mussel Ridge. In no time at all an inlet opened up on our right. I eased up on the throttle and turned into it.

"Thribry diyja Sup Urg Rigit?" Roy sputtered as he tried to make himself understood through the remains of his White Owl. He stuck his finger in his mouth, gutted and discarded the remains, and wiped his chin. "Think this is the St. George River?" he asked sardonically.

"What else could it be?" I responded in kind, and turned upriver.

"Don't look very big," he observed, after we'd navigated the critically narrowing waterway around a few more bends.

Getting no response from me, he continued: "When I was a young fella we used to come to see the big seiners work the St. George for alewives. Don't seem possible that even the fish could have got up this little trickle, let alone the boats."

"Well, the tide is just about dead low," I offered by way of explanation, and jerked a thumb at the clamdiggers whose numbers and proximity were increasing as we crawled upstream.

"Tide'd hafta be bigger 'n Fundy to make this little dribble the river I remember," said Roy wryly, as he lit up a fresh White Owl.

By the time we rounded the next bend the beam of the whaler occupied nearly the entire width of the channel which, up ahead, disappeared completely under a little bridge set amid a few houses and small buildings. I slowed to a crawl.

"I know Thomaston's a small town," said Roy, "but it must've suffered a wicked decline to have come to this."

A clamdigger sloshed up to the side of the boat and, resting his arms on the gunwale, asked Roy for a light. The fact that he was able to accomplish this in spite of our boat still being in gear was not lost on me. I discreetly slipped her into neutral. "Where you boys headed?" he asked, mating the end of Roy's White Owl with his Camel.

"Thomaston," I replied confidently in spite of my diminishing conviction. I reminded myself that this was but a lowly clamdigger and I, for the moment at least, had command of a trickle-going vessel.

He gave the prospect the same thoughtful consideration that must have been elicited from a prospector in the Rockies when a family in a covered wagon responded to a similar inquiry, "Oregon."

"Well let me and the boys step back outta the way 'cause you're going to need to get up a helluva head of steam to clear that bridge yonder."

I wished that he would indeed step back, he and his companions, back to the shore, back to their pickup, back to their homes, and out of my situation, because I was certainly going to suffer further and more intense humiliation the longer I remained in their company. But Roy, untroubled, had by now poured our new acquaintance a drink and some of his friends had drawn closer. They were leaning on their forks and clearly enjoying this diversion.

"Well," I said, summoning my remaining cockiness and yet desperate to extricate myself, "we might try going back down river now, so if you boy's just step back a little——"

"Oh sure, sorry. Didn't mean to hold you up. Go right on ahead." He removed himself from the gunwale and glanced over his shoulder to satisfy himself that his companions were paying attention.

Tentatively applying a little throttle only produced a muffled groan as the two Mercs screwed themselves into the mud bottom. The growing awareness that my ordeal had not run its course consumed me.

I stepped close to Roy and spoke quietly to him. A moment later he gracefully eased his bulk over the side and into the water. The ballast thus jettisoned, a big sucking sound ensued as the muck belched and released its grip on the props.

The fact that the twenty or so clamdiggers were in stitches was making if difficult for me to retain my composure. One had fallen backward in hysterics and was pounding the mud around him with his fork. Standing next to the boat in a few inches of water, Roy was stoic in flip-flops, a pair of large bovine print Bermudas, his old Boy Scout leader's jacket complete with merit badges of every description, and a red baseball cap that read "Where the hell is Vinalhaven?" With one hand holding a new drink and the other folded behind his back he was a vision of dignity in the face of overwhelming odds.

I engaged the electric lift and raised the props out of the water. Offering a kind of closure, our companion spoke up again.

"Now, this here," jerking his head around in a kind of sweeping introduction, "is the Westkeag River. You're looking for the St. George. You turned to starboard one stream too soon. Matter fact, this time of year this really ain't hardly no stream at all. Most of this water you're navigating now is only the run-off from Gray Smith hosing down his tractor up there by the bridge which he does reg'lar on Mondays. Now I suggest you and Katherine Hepburn here," jerking a thumb at Roy, "abandon the *African Queen* for a spell and go up to the 'Gig'; that's the little store yonder, and get you some lunch. For that matter, you could get a room up to the

Weskeag Inn and just live out the rest of your days if'n you never want your faces seen back home again. On the other hand, if you got no pride at all, you could wait here with me and the boys for the tide which, incidentally, is still goin'. Probably be three hours or so till the incomin' reaches your boat and you get a chance to hightail it outta here."

As I couldn't bear the thought of being the object of their amusement a moment longer than I had to, I humbly suggested an alternative. "It looks like this stream is nearly as wide as the boat is long. Maybe we could turn her around with the help of you and some of your friends and let it carry us back downstream."

Wordlessly Roy reached into the boat and pulled out a bag of plastic cups. He lined up a dozen or so on the gunwale and began filling them from his cooler.

A few minutes later we were facing downstream, but not in enough water to lower the props. I stood in the mud on one side and Roy on the other and we walked the boat down river. Our newfound acquaintances remained behind, basking in the wonderful sense of renewal that a good rollicking laugh provides. As we rounded the bend that put them out of view we could hear the dwindling strains of the old spiritual "Wade in the Water" being passably rendered by this good-natured group. In an hour or so we reached the ocean and climbed back aboard. Roy sat on the gunwale and rinsed off his legs and flip flops and resumed his station to my left at the console. He looked exactly as he had when he'd first come aboard hours earlier. I was a mess. My sneakers and socks and my jeans to the thighs were covered with mud. Everywhere I stepped, I oozed mud out onto the deck.

Roy lit up a fresh White Owl and poured a new drink. Exiting the mouth of the estuary we took a right. Up ahead lay ledges, islands, nuns, cans, a lobster boat and no course obvious to us. We approached the lobster boat slowly so as not to create a wake. The sole occupant was bent over a trap. His long, low wooden boat rode low as though water logged. The gunwales were covered with gull droppings, gurry, and dried brown spots. The exhaust and muffler sticking up through the cabin roof were sufficiently rotten to emit a low rumble as the boat idled. The old lobsterman was tending his work to starboard as we approached the aft port quarter, reversing to stop our forward progress. He caught sight of us in his peripheral vision. Startled, he jerked upright. I guess the thing that caught his attention above all else was Roy's Boy Scout jacket with its badges and emblems. Must have looked like a warden's jacket for a brief moment or so. With a younger man's grace he reached beneath the gunwale, retrieved a scaling basket, and flung it overboard. As it arched toward the surface the lobsters fell out spreading their *short* claws as if trying to gain some purchase.

In the moment that followed he realized Roy wasn't a warden and his relief matched our chagrin. "Howdy," I smiled, wanting to gain the advantage and conclude our business before the impact of his loss had its full effect.

He nodded acknowledgement.

"How do I get to the St. George River?"

He looked at me as if I had asked him which way was up and spat some residual tobacco juice onto his gunwale. He jerked a thumb over his shoulder, "See that smoke over't sou'west?"

We did.

"Thomaston dump," he declared. "Head straight for it till you get to the river. Can't miss it."

"Thank you kindly," I offered.

"No problem. Say, how's the taters this year?"

"Taters?"

"Yeah, you know, potatoes."

"Potatoes?" I repeatedly stupidly.

"Christ yes, potatoes! You boys is from up in 'Roostik' ain't ya?" (He was referring to Maine's northernmost county, famous for potatoes and farmers who'd never set foot in a boat. He had managed admirably to restrain himself up to this point, but the genius he attributed to his own humor and the subtlety with which he perceived its deliverance overcame him and he doubled over in such laughter that it drowned out the sound of his idling and similarly unrestrained engine.

Humbled and unnoticed, we took our leave. Roy lit a new White Owl and puffed at it leisurely as I pursued a moderate course toward the columns of smoke. The St. George River arrived on the heels of my relief after we passed though the straits at Port Clyde.

"Little bigger, ain't it?" observed Roy.

It could have been the Nile. I eased the throttle forward and we roared upstream, my confidence returning in a rush. In no time we were at the Thomaston waterfront where the river doglegs dramatically to the left. To our right and quite close to the far shore stood a formidable monument. The described channel beyond left pitiful little room for navigation. Between this marker and the shore to our left, however, lay a considerable expanse of water. Hardly throttling back at all I turned sharply to pursue this obviously preferable course. The force with which we struck soft bottom for the second time that day caused me to fly over the console, the windshield, and the bow and land in a foot or so of water. Unhurt, I struggled to my feet. Roy remained at the console, where he had been bracing himself with both hands as we had taken the speedy turn. The rooster tail we had moments before been displaying to such effect had followed up and over the suddenly motionless boat and had dampened his cigar but not his spirits. The engines were stalled. My feet were stuck and I was sinking in the mud. Work on the nearby shore had stopped and observers were gathering. A Thomaston lobsterboat cruised alongside casually and reversed to a stop not two feet from our boat. The captain emptied his corncob and refilled it from a pouch of Carter Hall drawn from his oil pants while he looked us over. "Aground ain't ya?" he queried dryly.

Roy poured a drink and sauntered to the stern to offer it to the lobsterman. He took it and they talked in low tones, broken by an occasional chuckle. Eventually they finished their drinks. The water was at my chest. The lobsterman tossed a coil of pot warp in my direction and wrapped the other end around the davit. "Hold on," he instructed.

Someday a diver exploring the bottom there will wonder at the circumstances that came to a pair of size 13 Reeboks standing casually side by side as if awaiting the return of someone who didn't want to track mud into the house.

⚓⚓⚓

Ask Not What Your Government Can Do for You

I have two ladies working for me at the motel. Capable and devoted, they've been with me for years. My government, specifically the Department of Justice, has unexpectedly asked, after all this time, for my assurance that neither Betsy or Roseann is an alien. I must demonstrate, to their satisfaction, that neither waded across the Rio Grande last night thus denying meaningful employment to the many good God-fearing Americans who are beating down my door looking for a chance to clean rooms at the Tidewater.

The announcement came from the Immigration and Naturalization Service (INS). I've grown suspicious of government agencies and particularly of those who find it necessary to remind themselves and us that they exist to serve. Still there's abundant evidence to suggest no number of reminders would be too many. The Internal Revenue *Service,* the Maine State Ferry *Service,* and the National Marine Fisheries *Service* come to mind. Lest a troubled employee be among my readers, I hasten to add that there are exceptional people at each agency. You know who you are and so do we.

The information packet I received from the INS is a bound blue pamphlet. It measures 10½ by 13, two inches larger than conventional printed material, so it won't fit in a normal envelope. I took it back to the Post Office—which, in a worrisome turn, not long ago changed its name to the U.S. Postal *Service*—to have it weighed. One and a quarter pounds, same as a good eating lobster. The cover introduces the contents, *You and the INS, Avoiding Problems before They Sneak across the Border.* The inside cover instructs the reader that, in accordance with the Paperwork Reduction Act, all government agencies are required to inform the reader of the estimated time required to read and absorb the enclosed material; in this case, eighteen hours and twelve minutes. As I ponder that disclosure my attention is drawn to the penalty for noncompliance, $10,000 a day for every day I am found to be thus. And "noncompliance" doesn't mean having *hired* alien workers. It means having failed to demonstrate that I *haven't* done so, a wild corruption of my presumed right to innocence until proven guilty. Skimming over the information, I learn that the empowering legislation had gone into effect a month before I became aware of it. Hence, I was already in a condition of noncompliance and apparently liable for fines of up to $300,000 or so. I thought it best to call the INS directly and put things right, since $300,000 was nearly all I had budgeted that year for fines and penalties. I dialed the 800 number on the back page inviting me to call with comments or questions, or for information. The answering recording informed me that I had, indeed, dialed the right number and it confirmed their hours of operation, within which I was calling, prompting me to wonder at the redundancy and waste of time in confirming the obvious. The message went on to inform me of their location and then offered me a menu of options from which to choose. I listened for the chance to talk to someone human about my noncompliant circumstances but there was no such menu item. Neither did a warm body ever come on the line, nor was there any indication one eventually would. I called my senator's office to find out how I could talk to a real person about my situation and was told that the INS had an office in Portland but that its number was unlisted. They did, however, give me the number. I dialed it.

If this isn't exactly the message played by the answering machine it's close enough:

"You have reached the Portland office of the Immigration and Naturalization Service. Our hours of operation are Monday through Friday 9:00 A.M. to 4:00 P.M. Our offices are located at 739 Warren Ave and our telephone is unpublished, as you by now know, so you should feel good about yourself for having gotten this far. If you are an employer and you suspect an employee of being an alien, push 1 and he or she will be terminated. If you suspect a competitor of hiring illegal aliens, and if reporting that competitor to us will make you feel patriotic, push 2 and we will visit the business in question. If you would like information regarding the reissuance of a green card, push 3. If you are an illegal alien and feel you have been denied employment based on your race, sex, or national origin, push 4. If you have pushed 4 and are willing to turn yourself in to be deported, push 5. If you are not an illegal alien but feel you have been denied employment because of your sex, race or national origin, push 6. If you are not an illegal alien but have been denied employment because someone thought you looked like one, push 7. If you are Islamic push 8. For all other inquiries remain on the line. This menu will now be repeated in Creole."

I never did talk to anyone at that office, but I did conduct a thorough interrogation of Betsy and Roseann and satisfied myself that they were not aliens. I wrote the INS of my assurance and offered as further evidence the fact that Betsy's father used to work for my father and that Roseanne and I went to school together and I once wrecked my car in her front yard and her folks came out and pulled me from the wreckage. So far I haven't heard from the INS so they must have been satisfied with my response; otherwise, at $10,000 a day times for four months, well, I'm over budget.

One year, during a slow period, Betsy went to work part-time at the local lobster-processing plant to augment the apparently inadequate wages she made working for me. After a while things slowed down at the plant, too, and she was laid off, although she continued to work for me as she had without interruption for years. Having lost the supplemental income from the plant, she applied for partial unemployment benefits. When I got my next quarterly assessment from the Deptartment of Labor, Job *Service,* I discovered we'd been assigned a penalty. I called the department to find out why.

"Because," I was told, "you laid off Betsy."

"What makes you think I laid off Betsy?"

"Betsy was laid off and she listed you as her employer on her application for benefits," responded the long-suffering agent.

"Could I trouble you to produce the document in question so we can review it over the phone?"

Clearly oppressed, this state employee, probably tenured and secure and subsequently not at all mindful of her obligations as a servant of the people, acquiesced. "Right here on line four she has written the date she was laid off."

"And where does it say *I* laid her off?"

"It asks her to name her employer and she names you."

"Well, I *am* her employer, have been for years, was on the day she filled out that form, and continue to be."

"Well then, who laid her off?"

"Well, as it happens I know who laid her off," and I named the fish plant and explained the part-time nature of her employment.

"Well, she should have said so. We just assume the employer she lists is the one responsible for laying her off."

"Perhaps you need to redesign your form to allow for the many folks in this state who work more than one job to make ends meet, so they can make it abundantly clear, even to you, that their loyal employer and the one that laid them off are not one in the same. At any rate, I am not the responsible employer. Would you please reverse the penalty?"

"You'll have to file an appeal," replied the still suffering and greatly inconvenienced agent. "I'll send you a form."

"How about if I just let you talk to Betsy and she will confirm what I have told you and you can reassign the penalty to the proper employer?"

That would not be possible, it was explained to me. The promised form, an application for an administrative appeal, arrived soon with an admonishment to file it within fifteen days or lose my right to appeal. I filed it, explaining the circumstances. Three weeks later I received a notice to appear before the Administrative Board of Appeals in Augusta at 8:30 A.M. on a day in August. I was to be armed with documentation supporting the grounds for my appeal and should present myself with the subject employee in tow. Such an appearance, of course, means taking the ferry to the mainland the night before, staying in a motel, driving to Augusta, staying who knows how long for the hearing, and making it back to Rockland to catch the last boat to Vinalhaven that night. August was not a good time for me and half my staff of two to take two days off. I called Augusta, explained the inconvenient timing, and was invited to appeal the decision to schedule an appeal. I did and the department offered to schedule a hearing in Rockland at a later date when all the hearing officers could be there. A few weeks later a notice arrived informing me of an appeal, scheduled for my convenience, in Rockland on September 15, a day I was, unfortunately, expected in Connecticut to visit family. I called the Augusta office and explained the conflict. Having made this effort to be accommodating, they were very put out with me. With trepidation, I explained to them that the inconvenience was at least partly mine since it was their mistake that had produced the confusion in the first place. Reluctantly, they agreed to give me an opportunity to appeal the decision to schedule an alternative date to hear my appeal. I did and was soon informed of a date several months hence, which worked for everyone.

The date arrived, but by then I had forgotten it. The Appeals Board had not however, and had assembled in Rockland. I was not there, neither was my supporting documentation; needless to say, nor did I have the subject employee in tow. A notice arrived a few days later informing me that by having failed to appear I had forfeited my right to appeal. In small print at the bottom of the page, however, I noticed that I did have an additional fifteen days to appeal this latest decision refusing my right to appeal the earlier decision. I availed myself of this opportunity, and in response the department informed me that the appeal would be conducted via a conference telephone call at a date we all agreed on a month or so hence. The agreed-upon date arrived. I forgot again, of course, but at the appointed hour the phone rang. On the other end were three appeals officials in three different locations around the state and a state referee in Augusta. On this end was my wife who, although she was dimly aware of the mistakenly applied penalty and how it had come to be, had not been kept apprised of developments, was not expecting this call, and was in the motel lobby checking in a couple of young guys. The referee impatiently informed her of the reason for the hearing, and Elaine arranged for the conference operator to call Betsy, the employee in question, blissfully unaware and at home. Betsy became the fifth participant. The referee started things off by beginning a recitation of events leading up to this moment, but was soon distracted by the sound of little fingers practicing the piano.

"Where is that piano noise coming from?" asked the referee.

"That's my daughter at her piano lesson," replied Betsy.

"Well, please tell her to stop for as long as it takes us to conclude this hearing."

"I pay good money for these lessons and it takes every ounce of persuasion I can muster to get her to stick to it. I'm not going to tell her to stop."

"Then please pick up another phone or take a portable to another room."

"I don't have another phone or a portable but I can stretch this cord out till it reaches the attic stairs and I can sit in there on the step."

She did so. The referee then continued to the muted accompaniment of Pachabel's Canon: "Betsy, please state your full name and address, raise your right hand and swear that the testimony you are about to give is the truth, the whole truth and nothing but the truth, so help you God. Elaine, you will please do the same."

They did and each solemnly intoned, "I do."

"Let the record show they have both been duly sworn. Elaine, would you please tell the assembled hearing what circumstances led to your husband's having failed to appear at the August hearing at which time his appeal of the denial of his appeal of the denial of his appeal of the penalty assignment for having terminated Betsy was to have been heard?"

"He forgot."

A long pause. "Is that all?"

"Course that's all," offered Betsy. "He forgets everything. Shouldn't come as any surprise he'd forget a meeting with you folks."

Another long pause. "Do either of you have anything further to contribute?"

"Can I put my hand down now?" asked Betsy.

The referee ignored the request. "Do any of the hearing officers have questions?"

Bobby, the proprietor of Port of Call Hardware, glanced across the street. He noticed that Elaine had her hand up and was being confronted by a couple of guys. Apparently she was being robbed. He raced across the street with the only weapon he could find, his squirt gun. Maybe he could bluff 'em. The assembled hearing officials heard him burst through the door demanding, "Up against the wall, both of you, turn around and don't try anything funny. Elaine, you OK?" The bluff worked and while they stood, compliant, Elaine lowered her hand and explained the situation.

"Hearing no further questions and there being no objection, I declare this hearing concluded. A summary of findings will be forwarded to all parties within thirty days."

Accordingly, I was soon informed that my appeal of the decision to deny my appeal of the decision to deny my appeal of the decision to assign my business the other business's penalty was denied and no further recourse was available to me.

Of course, they didn't know about this book.

⚓⚓⚓

The Great American Duck Race

The year 2002 marked the tenth consecutive Great American Duck Mill Race. The race is dependent upon the tide, which an hour or two after slack water is surging into the Carver's Pond estuary at a clip sufficient to give the red, yellow, blue, and green plastic ducks a good head of steam as they converge on the illusive finish line, an elusive spot existing only in the mind and eye of whoever has the fortitude to serve as judge.

This has always been the purest form of undertaking. Volunteers from the organizations who will profit from the event staff the sales booth for a week or so beforehand selling tickets at five dollars each. The beneficiary this year was the Babe Ruth Baseball League, and the young men ensconced therein (except for a brief interlude when two scantily clad and somewhat more worldly girls of about the same vintage sidled up to either side of the booth and questioned the boys as to their age and inclinations) worked enthusiastically to net three thousand dollars, which will be divided between the league and playground.

The ascribed purity, however, has ended. As proprietor of the Paper Store that sits astride the Millstream like a five-hundred-pound gorilla (not the proprietor, the Paper Store), and whose command of the adjacent waterway can hardly be ignored, Carlene Michael, pretender to the Board of Selectmen (see "Shades of 2000") is always in charge of the race. This year, because I'm a good sport and in spite of having been denied by her and by fraudulent election proceedings my rightful place on the Board of Selectmen, I was willing to bury the hatchet in the interest of the greater good. Accordingly, as before, I hung the banner announcing the race. Likewise I volunteered to serve again, paddling feverishly around in the current and eddies, as retriever of "also ran" ducks.

I cannot find the words (actually I can't print the words) to describe my dismay when, among the ducks retrieved by my devoted bowman we discovered, with heavy hearts, my own blue (no. 131) duck, floating upside down, quite dead, with its tiny head split open and two tiny cinder blocks attached to its little webbed feet.

The message was not lost on me, but I am not intimidated and plan to run again.

⚓ ⚓ ⚓

Victoria Station

Has anyone noticed the *Victoria's Secret* catalogues are getting a little provocative? Woodrow McFadden has. He arrived just ahead of his wife, Emily, at the Post Office one day in September and it was almost worth it. Rifling through the chaff, he grabbed the *Victoria's Secret Swim* 2002 catalogue, tried to conceal it inside an *Eddie Bauer*, and headed for the door, leaving behind on the counter the electric bill, several other catalogues, a check from Delphine VanMiddlesworth for the caretaking he'd done that winter, and two notices from the IRS. One notice advised him that he'd underestimated his income in 2000, had therefore paid too little in quarterly estimated tax payments, and was now being assessed a penalty. The other advised him that in 2001 he'd overestimated and was being penalized for having paid too much. Emily was heading in the door just as Woodrow was headed out. Another minute or two and he'd have been in the truck, safely under way, and headed for the fish house, where he could examine the spring fashions at his leisure. It was not to be. The small *Eddie Bauer* couldn't contain the larger *Victoria's Secret* catalogue any more effectively than the tiny outfits therein contained the models upon whom they were so appealingly arranged. Emily snatched the catalogue from under his arm, delivered a withering look, and sent him back to the counter to pick up the real mail.

Recently I had occasion to make the mail run myself every day for an entire week; usually Elaine retrieves it. During that week nine different *Victoria's Secret* catalogues arrived. Unlike the ladies who graced the interior, each catalogue was a different shape. Every one, though, had a couple of things in common. Don't get ahead of me now. I'm talking about, for example, miracles. Miracles appear to be a common theme. Several miracle undergarments, each offering a different means of achieving miraculous results were modeled to great effect on young women whose need, individually, for a miracle was only marginally less urgent than Michael Jordan's need for shoe lifts. The miracle, if the ad copy is to be believed, can sometimes be accomplished by simply donning one of these delicate items and securing the fasteners. That act alone will apparently transform the wearer—providing she is a breathtakingly beautiful and nearly anorexic young woman to begin with—into, well, into a breathtakingly beautiful and nearly anorexic young woman who, clad like that, could sell bait bags to an astronaut. In other cases, the miracle is achieved by means of adjustable equipment. By manipulating a discreetly located little chain, the result can be modest miracles for modest moments, as when not too much encouragement is needed, or really big miracles for those occasions when, claims the ad, the young ladies in the catalogue find it necessary to bring all their resources to bare. The ad presumes, I guess, that somewhere out there among the heterosexual males exist some remarkably resistant individuals.

It's an interesting piece of marketing, this catalogue, and effective. Superficially it is designed to appeal to men. The cover girl is smiling invitingly, or at least looking coy. If the man picks up the mail, the *Victoria's* catalogue will therefore likely get taken home, and the competition, *Chadwick's, Nordstrom's,* the aforementioned *Eddie Bauer, Land's End,* and the rest will be discarded with the same wild abandon employed in sending a short lobster over the side. This, even though the models within, each presenting an appealing front as it were, are glaring sullenly with a scowl that effectively telegraphs the message "In your dreams, Bozo, you stand less of a chance with me than a snake's belly in a skidder's wheel rut." Such a bruising bait-and-switch encounter is an awful letdown after having made the acquaintance of the nice lady on the cover. No matter.

If the woman picks up the mail, on the other hand, *Chadwick's, Eddie Bauer,* and the like *do* get home but so does the *Victoria's Secret,* because women never throw out catalogues no matter what. I recently found myself in the bathroom thumbing through one titled *Memories of Vigor—A Catalogue of Enhancements for your Maturing Man.* Where did that come from and why on earth is she keeping it around?

Women thumb through the *Victoria's Secret* catalogue apparently oblivious to its tenuous perch on the fence separating soft sell from soft porn. But women thumb through *all* catalogues automatically. As their lungs instinctively draw in and expel air, as they have a convincing capacity for making their own ideas seem like his, as they peel through a sale rack more intuitively and effectively than John Ashcroft can flay through the Constitution, so do a woman's thumbs instinctively advance through the pages of a catalogue—any catalogue. And once inside they buy stuff, even from *Victoria's Secret,* because to buy stuff from a catalogue is as compelling as thumbing through it to begin with. The whole business is second nature to them. The glowering young ladies who wear their expressions like armor do not trouble them.

This fall we had the pleasure of hosting an L. L. Bean catalogue shoot here at the Tidewater. It was a huge undertaking. An enormous bus served as a makeup room, dressing room, communications center, snack bar, waiting (of which there was a great deal) room, and command post. Hairdressers were flown in from Boston, makeup people from New York, and dressmakers from the West Coast. The shoot lasted almost two weeks; the bus traveled all over the island, finding just the right spot to feature an attractive model in some article of Bean's clothing. All the team members were housed and fed here on the island. L. L. Bean found our island's beautiful shores and woodlands, lighthouses and quarries to be good settings for the photo shoot. Why wouldn't any catalogue feel similarly? Why wouldn't *Victoria's Secret?* Their catalogue makes such great use of water, the swimsuits and all, and here we are after all, a motel right in the ocean. Imagine Tyra Banks, Heidi Klum, and Laetitia Casta frolicking right here in the Millstream. I could put pictures of them in my brochure. Of course, we'd have to keep them over in the west current, away from the overboard discharge. (I don't have those names memorized, incidentally; I had to look them up.)

⚓ ⚓ ⚓

Bunglaries

Every town has a Bubba. This fall our own version and his helpers, the Bubbarettes, undertook to rob a couple of island businesses. Typical of cyclical off-season capers, every few years for as long as I can remember, this one provided enough fodder to get us all through the winter.

During the planning stage, a brief period earlier in the day coinciding with the time it takes three guys to consume a pack of Bud, they settled on hitting the Fishermen's Friend, a convenience store, and the Tidewater Motel, each on the north shore of Carver's Harbor, and they seized on an imaginative means of gaining entry. They would bust out some windows.

It's not unusual out here to be awoken late at night or in the predawn morning by the sound of squealing tires or mufflers beyond their prime. Neither is it unusual to ignore such interruptions and try to go back to sleep, since calls to the sheriff would only mean two people are now trying to get back to sleep. No doubt the resourceful perpetrators had this in mind when they roared into the parking lot of Fisherman's Friend around two o'clock in the morning, the din of empties bouncing around in the back of Bubba's truck competing with the warlike rumble coming from the exhaust pipe that led from the engine block toward, but not quite to, the space where the muffler used to be.

I confess I'm being a little sarcastic, reluctant to give credit for the modest level of sophistication the operation actually achieved. In fact some thought *had* gone into the planning of this enterprise. Earlier in the day, for example, the trio had unobtrusively reviewed the parade of punts occupying the float at the lobster wharf, adjacent to Fisherman's Friend, and returning to a conference in the pickup, agreed on one in particular which would suit their needs that night, one that looked to be in good shape, i.e., not swamped, and in which the oars had been left, a vessel in which they could vanish into the black night with their booty. For some reason that has escaped investigators but must have made sense to the bunglers, the skiff seemed somehow a means of making off with the loot preferable to just throwing stuff in the truck and driving off. Accordingly, then, the first order of business later that night was for one of them to retrieve said punt, row it over to Fishermen's Friend, and position it directly under the wharf, which, in turn, was directly beneath the aforementioned window. This task was assigned to one of the apprentices who, having seen a few old westerns but not having spent much time on the water—not enough anyway—simply tossed the line around a piling in what was nearly, but not quite, a half hitch and climbed the ladder to help with stage two.

Approaching the window with a few rocks, the value of tireless planning again reluctantly acknowledged, they took off their T-shirts, wrapped them around the stones, and smashed out the window. The T-shirts muffled the sound of rock against glass, but a moment later they were startled nearly to sobriety by an apparent answering gunshot until they realized that a residual rock they'd tossed overboard had struck the blade of one of the improperly shipped oars. What they hadn't noticed was that the discarded stone caused the struck oar to catapult itself out of the rowboat and, the north wind having picked up, make for the opposite shore. Eager to get inside and at the goods, they began pulling out the remaining shards of glass and while so doing made the shrewd and uncharacteristically collective observation that the window was, in fact, not a functioning window at all but simply a storm panel barely nailed over an opening. A few fingers positioned themselves around the perimeter and it popped right out.

Inside, they made first for the beer cooler and executed the efficient removal of its contents to the punt. Planning and its product priorities uppermost, Bubba number one ran all the Budweiser to the window; Bubba number two to the wharf's edge, where number three, lying on his stomach, lowered each six pack gently, to avoid aggravating its effervescence, but quickly to the punt bobbing below just at arm's length in the quickening northerly breeze. Their drink of choice exhausted and following a modest debate on the merits of Bud versus the deficiencies of some of the remaining stock, the group condescended to add a few cases of Shipyard and Michelob. These, they reasoned, could be offered to the less discriminating and all too frequent guests back at Bubba's.

Done with phase one, they concentrated their meager resources on the removal of less fragile commodities. Cartons of cigarettes went flying, along with the finesse they'd employed in delicately removing the beer, out the window and over the side in the direction of the empty space where the punt had, until the gathering northerly relaxed its tenuous tether on the piling, been docked. Now, though, unbeknownst to them and with a decided list due to the excess Bud stowed to port, it was chasing its prodigal oar across the harbor.

The store's trash-can liner was freed of its contents and into it they dumped the lottery tickets they'd unreeled from the countertop dispenser, single packs of cigarettes raked from the wall rack, and all the candy bars they could gather. Loosely knotted, the bag went blithely over the side to join the smokes heading south.

Any patron of the Fishermen's Friend knows the location of the safe and these guys were no exception. Having decided, wisely, against dropping it into the presumed punt, they opted for pulling and tugging the big two-by-three-foot, several-hundred-pound vault to the front door and wrestling it outside. There they found themselves flatteringly but unfavorably illuminated by the store's big spotlight and the several neon window signs summoning the consumer's attention to merchandise, much of which, thanks to these three, was no longer available. Unable to get the safe up into the bed of the truck, they dragged it, using scavenged boards and rope, through and among the shadows of hulls cradled at adjacent Hopkin's Boat Yard until, much later, they arrived at a spot on the shore which afforded what they felt was enough privacy for them to begin the delicate removal of its contents, sure to be cash and more lottery tickets. Nearby they found a plentiful supply of their weapon of choice, big rocks, and began raining these down on the safe's door, which, had they spent the last two hours dragging it in any other position but on its back, would have fallen open of its own volition as it was not locked and never had been. After a while one of the trio was dispatched to take command of the expected punt and embark on a course that would take him and the vessel to a designated spot over on Lanes Island, a place they hoped would afford them the later luxury of retrieving the goods undetected. His abrupt return dampened their spirits, but the news that the punt and its laboriously secured contents were gone settled over them like a great beer-soaked blanket. Frustrated that so much had gone wrong in so short a period of time, Bubba picked up a piece of angle iron and took a great swipe at the safe, inadvertently wedging the iron under the handle, which, when he tried to jerk it free, lifted enough to reveal, even to these three, that the door was already open. The anticipated cash and lottery tickets stuffed into their shirts and pants, and, their spirits buoyed, they made good their getaway and headed uptown.

At the motel, eager to make up their losses, they busted out an awning window that was much too small for any one of them to have squeezed through before trying the door and finding it open. Bubba ripped the cash register from its mooring, carried it out into Main Street in the advancing light of dawn, and in full view of several fishermen heading down to the shore, and cradling it like a newborn, marched to the truck, mysteriously parked nearly a hundred yards away. There they discovered that the register, too, was already open, and accordingly they relieved it of its contents, a couple hundred dollars.

The gossip is that the miscreants were all eventually apprehended. We've received no official notification even though we own the violated motel. Neither have the proprietors of the Fishermen's Friend. Apparently, the Knox County sheriff felt we had "no need to know." As a result of this experience we, not surprisingly, began retrieving the money and locking the lobby door each night. Quite a few folks, though, encouraged us to resume our old practice of leaving the money in the register and the lobby door open. They even provided a surveillance camera and said they'd chip in and compensate us if we were hit again. They thought it would be worth it just to view the film.

⚓⚓⚓

Mainland Security

The Constitution of the United States contains no provision for its arbitrary modification. Fortunately, however, the Framers, apparently recognizing the value of a little interpretive latitude, inserted occasional language allowing for the exercise of broad license now and then. Specifically, for example, the Fourth Amendment guarantees our right to be secure against search, but only *unreasonable* search. In qualifying search as "unreasonable," however, the constitution allows for liberal interpretation. The Framers would agree, I guess, that whether a search is "reasonable" is a question best decided by the president or by the attorney general.

The separation of powers has been interpreted—an interpretation recently upheld by the Fourth U.S. Circuit Court of Appeals—as meaning that our constitutional protections are sacred only to a point. That juncture, in this case, is when the application of those constitutional protections handicaps the president in exercising his inclination to act as judge and jury and to declare American citizens, arrested on American soil, enemy combatants unworthy of constitutional protections, who can be held indefinitely without being charged, and whose access, even supervised, to an attorney or to his or her own family would jeopardize national security.

AND SO.

Whereas these islands and the inhabitants thereof are the first line of defense if the enemy (an Arab for example) is approaching from the East, those seeking passage thereto will be subject to the rules and regulations published in TER-RORISTS ARE ALL FROM AWAY, SO PEOPLE FROM AWAY ARE ALL SUSPECT, a publication of the newly formed Department of Mainland Security. This informative pamphlet is available from any ticket agent. Please take the time to read it care-fully. Give yourself plenty of time. The Paperwork Reduc-tion Act requires you be notified that it is expected to take three days to read and absorb the whole thing. A synopsis of its major provisions follows.

GENERAL

1. People from Away will no longer be allowed on the ferry. People from really Far Away, and recognizable by the presence of turbans, burkas, olives, lambs, date fronds, fil-terless cigarettes, facial stubble, or the Koran will be taken into custody and dispatched, as enemy combatants, to Matinicus, where they will be denied, in perpetuity, access, even supervised access, to legal representation or to family. Likewise, anyone in the vicinity during the aforementioned apprehension who is inadvertently swept up in the process will be similarly declared an enemy combatant, just in case.

In either event the taxpayers will be spared the expense of proving otherwise.

2. Other preventative measures put in place include closed-circuit television monitoring devices, both sound and audio, throughout the aptly named "terminal premises." The activities of everyone, including those in the "terminal restrooms," will be broadcast live to the large monitor in the "terminal waiting room." Extraordinary times call for extraordinary measures.

3. The Mainland Security Force, comprised of employees of the Maine State Ferry Service (MSFS) and reenforced by deputies from the Knox County Sheriff's Department, have been and continue to be thoroughly trained and will facilitate the imposition of security measures commensurate with levels of security threats imposed, from time to time, by the attorney general or the secretary of Homeland Security, the chief of Mainland Security (whose identity and location are undisclosed and whose number is unlisted) or the manager of the Maine State Ferry Service, according to the following color-coded levels of threat:

CODE	RESPONDENT
Blush	Knox County Detective
Mauve	Ticket Agents
Taupe	Line Attendants
Buff	Able-Bodied Seamen and Sheriff's Deputies
Aquamarine	Captains
Drab	The Sheriff

4. The aforementioned training is, as has been explained, ongoing. As a result, unannounced drills will take place from time to time. If, while you are here at the terminal going about your business or waiting in your vehicle for instructions, a drill commences, it would be helpful if you would assume the role of an Arab posing a threat or, if you are a family or group, the role of a bunch of Arabs posing a threat. Your cooperation will enhance the reality of the exercise and the result, your own consequent condition notwithstanding, will be a better-prepared Mainland Security Force, greater protection for us all and a coupon redeemable by survivors for a few moments of unrecorded privacy in the "terminal restroom."

5. Certain of the newly instituted security measures, such as the grenade launcher carried by the line attendant, will be obvious to you. The behavior of MSFS employees on other occasions, while thought-provoking, may or may not be a component of a security measure. It is best to assume the former and not to report a MSFS employee or someone you assume is an MSFS employee, regardless of his or her behavior. What you have witnessed may simply be an undisclosed security measure authorized surreptitiously by the Department of Mainland Security.

6. Above all, report anyone you feel is acting suspiciously or otherwise represents a threat to you or to others. Those people, even if they appear to be doing nothing more than simply occupying a vehicle ahead of you in line, the removal of which will increase your own chances of getting on the boat, will be apprehended by the Mainland Security Force and taken to an undisclosed location.

VEHICLES

1. Vehicles seeking passage to Vinalhaven must be in the Vinalhaven Line. Vehicles bound for Vinalhaven that are found, mistakenly or otherwise, to be in the North Haven Line will be sent to North Haven without recourse.

2. The drivers and all occupants of vehicles in the North Haven Line are assumed to be family of or acquaintances of or attorneys for the community of enemy combatants who comprise the North Haven community. All, once they step ashore on North Haven, are consigned to the island in perpetuity as enemy combatants and can only be released if a family member or attorney agrees to assume responsibility for them.

3. Family members and attorneys of and for enemy combatants will be assumed to be enemy combatants, and none from the original group of enemy combatants is allowed contact of any kind with the second group of enemy combatants, and the reverse is also true.

4. "Line cars" and the cars for which they are "holding a place" must be driven simultaneously by the same individual, who may not exit either vehicle at any time for any reason.

5. No individual will be allowed to drive a vehicle onto the ferry or to drive on terminal property or in the vicinity unless he/she has undergone a strip search by the line attendant.

6. Strip searches will be conducted by the line attendant on the stage at the Taxi Stand, hereinafter designated as the

terminal Reviewing Stand, one hour before each departure, unless the line attendant is, at the designated moment, shooting those who exited their vehicle without permission. In such an event, a Knox County Deputy, hereinafter referred to as the Line Attendant's Deputy, may conduct the strip search.

7. Strip searches are open to the public. Tickets may be purchased from the ticket agent and are nonrefundable, so be advised that you should review carefully the list of folks scheduled to be strip searched to be sure it's something you are going to enjoy.

8. No material will be transported in any vehicle that is not the property of an occupant of that vehicle. The driver of a BMW, when asked by the line attendant, "I see the Auto Parts Store just delivered a radiator to your car. Would that be your radiator?" must be able to answer convincingly, "Yes, I plan on turning it into a planter." If during a search, belongings are unearthed, such as a returning college student's typical stuff, the identity of which cannot be ascertained, or the ownership of which cannot be proven, or the alleged ownership of which seems unlikely, the senior officer of the Mainland Security Force may direct the deportation of the suspect individual or individuals to Matinicus or, for lesser offenses, to North Haven, or may, at the officer's discretion, simply have the suspect or suspects executed.

Note: Tickets must be held in the ticket holder's mouth and will be taken ONLY from the ticket holder's mouth. A saliva-laden ticket is the only means we have of guaranteeing a satisfactory sample of DNA.